Book C

LANGUAGE
Power

D0851598

gagelearning

Copyright © 2002 Gage Learning Corporation

164 Commander Blvd., Toronto, ON M1S 3C7

Adapted from material developed, designed, and copyrighted by Steck-Vaughn.

We acknowledge the financial support of the Government of Canada through the Book Publishing Industry Development Program for our publishing activities.

We acknowledge the Government of Ontario through the Ontario Media Development Corporation's Ontario Book Initiative.

Editorial Team: Chelsea Donaldson, Carol Waldock
Cover Adaptation: Christine Dandurand

ISBN **0-7715-1015-2**

10 MP 04 03
Printed and bound in Canada

Table of Contents

Unit 6 Study Skills

Final Reviews

Synonyms

> - A **synonym** is a word that has the same or nearly the same meaning as one or more other words.
>   EXAMPLES: help - aid - assist, cold - chilly - wintry

A. Write one synonym for each word below. Write another synonym in a short phrase. Underline the synonym in the phrase.

1. small — little — <u>tiny</u> bug
2. enormous — huge ✓ — <u>big</u> tree ✓
3. vehicle — automobile ✓ — <u>big</u> truck thing ✓ *phrase*
4. select — pick ✓ — <u>chose</u> one
5. complete — done ✓ — <u>finish</u> the race ✓
6. river — (stream) — <u>water</u> way
7. permit — allow ✓ — <u>agree</u> to ✓
8. speedy — speed ✓ — fast (rabbit) ✓

B. For each word in parentheses, write a synonym in the blank.

1. Many trees in an old forest are (high) __lofty__ ✓ .
2. Underneath them grow (lower) __below__ trees and plants. ✗
3. As the (aged) __older__ trees die, they make room for others. ✓
4. Sometimes fires will (destroy) __elimenates__ the entire forest.
5. Then from the (charred) __scorched__ earth sprout new plants.
6. They all begin their (stretch) __reach__ for the sky again.

C. Write three sentences about the forest. In each sentence, use a synonym for one of the words below. Underline the synonym.

~~begin~~	~~lofty~~	~~soil~~

punctuation

1. The seeds start to grow to grow.
2. Most trees are high P up.
3. The dirt in the forest is damp.

Capital letter?

Lesson 2 — Antonyms

> ■ An **antonym** is a word that has the opposite meaning of another word.   EXAMPLES: hot - cold, tall - short

A. Write an antonym for the underlined word in each phrase below.

1. dark blue _light blue_
2. busy worker _lazy worker_ (sp)
3. up the hill _down the hill_
4. noisy play _quiet play_
5. north wind _south wind_
6. buy a car _sell a car_
7. time of day _time of night_
8. bitter taste _sweet taste_
9. come now _go now_
10. good dog _bad dog_
11. small bird _big bird_
12. rough road _smooth road_ (sp)
13. black coat _white coat_
14. above the neck _below the neck_

15. frowning face _happy face_
16. under the bridge _over bridge_
17. pretty colour _ugly colour_ (sp)
18. cold water _hot water_
19. feeling strong _feeling week_ (sp)
20. wide belt _thin belt_
21. unhappy face _happy face_
22. east side _west side_
23. cool breeze _warm breeze_
24. stop the car _drive_
25. heavy jacket _lite jacket_
26. long story _short story_
27. give a gift _receive a gift_ (sp)
28. difficult task _easy task_

B. For each word in parentheses, write an antonym in the blank.

We were very (sad) _happy_ to be on vacation. It was the (last) _first_ time we had been able to (stay) _go_ in a long time, and this one would be really (boring) _fun_. We rented a (large) _small_ cabin near Whistler Mountain in B.C. We were hoping for (hot) _cold_ and snowy weather so we could ski. The (last) _first_ thing we did when we got to the cabin was (pack) _unpack_ our clothes. Then we hiked around (inside) _outside_. We liked being in such a (terrible) _wonderful_ (sp) place.

Homonyms

> ■ **Homonyms** are words that are pronounced alike but are spelled differently and have different meanings.
> EXAMPLES: I'll - aisle   two - too - to

A. Write a short phrase that includes a homonym for each word below. Circle each homonym.

1. haul ___long (hall)___ ✓

2. road ___I (rode) my bike___

3. sum ___(some) people are mean.___

4. way ___I (weigh) 80 lbs___

5. new ___I (knew) that___

6. meat ___I don't want to (meat) my mom's boss.___

> ■ Two is a number. Too means "also," "besides," or "more than enough." To means "toward." It is also used with such words as be, sing, play, and other action words.

B. Fill in the blanks with two, too, or to.

1. Ben was ___too___ ✓ frightened ___to___ ✓ utter a word.

2. He had heard the strange sound ___two___ ✓ times.

3. He went ___to___ his room upstairs, ___two___ steps at a time.
   But he heard it there, ___too___ ✓.

4. He decided ___to___ ✓ call his friend who lived ___two___ blocks away.
   It seemed the only thing ___to___ do!

> ■ Their means "belonging to them." There means "in that place." They're is a contraction of the words they are.

C. Underline the correct word in parentheses.

1. They are over (their, <u>there</u>, they're) standing in (<u>their</u>, there, they're) yard.

2. (Their, There, <u>They're</u>) waiting to go visit (<u>their</u>, there, they're) friends.

3. (Their, There, <u>They're</u>) going to leave for (their, <u>there</u>, they're) vacation.

■ Homographs are words that are spelled the same but have different meanings. They may also be pronounced differently.
EXAMPLE: <u>desert</u> meaning "a barren, dry place" and <u>desert</u> also meaning "to abandon"

A. Read each sentence and the two meanings for the underlined word. Circle the meaning that tells how the word is used in the sentence.

1. The soldiers' <u>arms</u> were old and rusty.
   a. parts of the body   (b.) weapons for war

2. Several had made <u>bats</u> from fallen tree limbs.
   a. flying mammals   (b.) rounded wooden clubs

3. The <u>long</u> war had made them all tired.
   (a.) extending over a considerable time   b. to wish for

4. They were all ready to go <u>back</u> home.
   a. part of the body   (b.) to a place from which a person came

5. They hoped someone would <u>lead</u> them to safety.
   a. soft, grey metal   (b.) to show the way

B. Write the homograph for each pair of meanings below. The first letter of each word is given for you.

1. a. sound made with fingers   b. a metal fastener   s snap

2. a. lame walk or step   b. not stiff   l azy

3. a. use oars to move a boat   b. a noisy fight   r ow

4. a. a tree covering   b. the sound a dog makes   b ark

5. a. to press flat   b. a yellow vegetable   s squash

C. Write pairs of sentences that show two different meanings for each homograph below. Use a dictionary if necessary.

1. school A school of fish. Algonquin School

2. pupil on an eye ball. A student

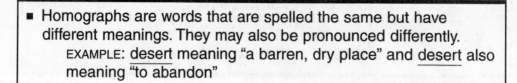

Prefixes and Suffixes

> - A **prefix** or a **suffix** added to a base word changes the meaning of the word.
>   EXAMPLE: re- meaning "again" + the base word <u>do</u> = <u>redo</u> meaning "to do again"
> - <u>Re-</u> means "again," <u>pre-</u> means "before," <u>mis-</u> means "wrongly" or "not," <u>-able</u> means "that can be," <u>-less</u> means "without," <u>-ness</u> means "state of being."

A. Write the word formed by each combination. Then write the definition of the new word.

1. kind + ness = _Kindness — not rude._

2. pre + date = _pre date — practice date._

3. help + less = _helpless — not able to move or do any thing_

4. re + made = _remade — did over_

B. Read each sentence. Use one of the prefixes or suffixes and the base word below each blank to form a new word. Write the new word in the blank.

> ~~mis-~~   ~~-ful~~   ~~pre-~~   -less   ~~re-~~   ~~-ness~~

1. Terry _relives_ her vacation by viewing the photographs
   (lives)
   she took.

2. She spends _endless_ hours enjoying the mountain scenery.
   (end)

3. Her favourite shot shows a mountain sunset just before
   darkness settled over their campsite.
   (dark)

4. John didn't see Terry's look of fright when a bear made
   a _predawn_ raid on the garbage can.
   (dawn)

5. John had _misread_ the camera directions in the dim light.
   (read)

6. He did, however, get a shot of the bear's _delightful_ cubs.
   (delight)

■ A **contraction** is a word formed by joining two other words. An apostrophe shows where a letter or letters have been left out.
EXAMPLES: it is = it's   we will = we'll

A. Write the contraction formed by the words.

1. who + is = _who's_

2. could + not = _couldn't_

3. they + have = _they've_

4. I + will = _I'll_

5. does + not = _doesn't_

6. should + have = _should've_

7. you + would = _you'd_

8. I + have = _I've_

9. that + is = _that's_

10. did + not = _didn't_

11. let + us = _let's_

12. they + are = _they're_

B. Use the contractions below to complete each sentence. Write the contractions on the lines.

| can't | couldn't | he'll | I'm | it's | I've | Let's |
| She's | wasn't | What'll | What's | Where's | | |

1. It _wasn't_ quite show time.

2. Kamal called out, "_What's_ Pearl?"

3. "What?" shouted Sara. "_it's_ not here yet?"

4. "No, and _I've_ looked everywhere."

5. "The show _can't_ go on without the star," Sara wailed.

6. Sara added, "_what'll_ we do?"

7. "_Let's_ ask Adam," Kamal suggested.

8. "Yes," said Sara, "_he'll_ know what to do."

9. Just then a voice called, "_where's_ all the excitement?"

10. "Pearl, _she's_ you!" Sara and Kamal exclaimed.

11. "Yes," said Pearl, "I know _I'm_ late."

12. Pearl added, "I _couldn't_ find my costume!"

Compound Words

> ■ **Compound words** may be two words written as one, two words joined by a hyphen, or two separate words.
> EXAMPLES: sunlight   ho-hum   easy chair

A. Draw a line between the two words that form each compound word below.

1. high/way
2. old/time
3. full/moon
4. snow/flake
5. air/conditioner

6. fire/drill
7. bare/foot
8. baby-sitter
9. splash/down
10. sweat/shirt

11. high/rise
12. earth/quake
13. half/mast
14. bull/dog
15. skate/board

B. Use two of the words below to form a compound word that will complete each numbered sentence. Write the word on the blank.

| after | back | come | hard | hood | neighbour | noon | out | ware | yard |

1. Jan and I bought a hammer and nails at a ___hardware___ store.
2. Part of the fence in our ___backyard___ was broken.
3. It took most of the ___afternoon___ to repair the fence.
4. We were proud of the ___outcome___.
5. Our fence was the finest in the ___neighbourhood___.

C. Use the second word part of each compound word to make the next compound word. Write the new word.

1. clubhouse   a building used by a club

   ___houseboat___   a boat that people can live in

   ___boathose___   a house for storing boats

2. teacup   a cup for drinking tea

   ___cupcake___   a cake the size of a cup

   ___cakewalk___   a circular walking game in which players may win a cake

Review

A. Write S before each pair of synonyms. Write A before each pair of antonyms. Write H before each pair of homonyms.

1. _A_ more, less
2. _S_ rich, wealthy
3. _A_ laugh, cry
4. _H_ cent, scent
5. _S_ neat, tidy

6. _A_ save, spend
7. _S_ late, tardy
8. _A_ sew, so
9. _H_ heel, heal
10. _S_ join, connect

11. _H_ steel, steal
12. _S_ certain, sure
13. _H_ wait, weight
14. _S_ false, untrue
15. _A_ refuse, accept

B. Write the correct homograph for the pair of lines in each sentence.

1. I found my red ink _____pen_____ in the dog's _____penn_____ .

2. Dropping the tennis _____racket_____ on the glass table made quite a _____racet_____ .

3. I couldn't _____bare_____ watching the _____bear_____ cub search for its mother.

4. It took a short time to _____ the building when it became _____ there was a fire.

5. When he said that to you, he didn't _____meen_____ to be _____mean_____ .

C. Add one of the following prefixes or suffixes to each underlined word to fit the meaning. Write the new word that is formed.

| re- | pre- | mis- | -ness | -able | -less |

1. to wire again _____re-wire_____
2. without hope _____hope-less_____
3. to soak before _____pre-soak_____
4. able to be washed _____wash-able_____
5. wrongly shapen _____mis-shapped_____
6. state of being good _____good-ness_____

7. without humour _____humour-less_____
8. to do again _____re-do_____
9. able to be removed _____remove-able_____
10. to view before _____re-view_____
11. state of being strange _____strange-ness_____
12. wrongly spelled _____mis spelled_____

D. Write the words that mean the same thing as the underlined contraction.

1. What's the reason the Franklins are moving? ~~Was~~ What is

2. They've decided the schools are better in Arthur. They have

3. I guess you'll get to go see their new house. You will

4. They told me I'd have to come visit soon. I would

5. Do the children think they'll like the new school? they will

E. Combine the words below to form six compound words. Write a sentence for each word on the lines.

back	night	loud	shore	tool	news
yard	sea	paper	time	speaker	box

1. My back-yard is not very big.
2. She sells seasheels by the sea-shore.
3. It's night-time, time for bed.
4. My dad has a tool-box.
5. My mom read the news-paper with her glass
6. The loud music is coming from a loud-speaker.

F. In the paragraph below, underline the contractions, and circle the compound words. Then write each marked word and the two words from which it is made on the lines.

I received a postcard from my friends. They will be travelling overseas in Europe throughout the summer. I believe that they're overdoing it. Why try to see everything in one trip?

1. overseas   over -seas
2. they're   they are
3. postcard   post-card
4. everything   every-thing
5. throughout   through-out
6. overdoing   over-doing

A. Read each phrase and the list of words beneath it. Write S before each word that is a synonym of the first word in the phrase. Write A before each word that is an antonym.

1. **break** a window

   _____ repair

   _____ shatter

   _____ mend

   _____ smash

2. **clean** air

   _____ pure

   _____ polluted

   _____ impure

   _____ fresh

3. **strong** legs

   _____ powerful

   _____ sturdy

   _____ weak

   _____ athletic

B. Choose a synonym or antonym from each of the three groups above. Write a sentence using each word.

1. _____

2. _____

3. _____

C. Use each pair of homonyms below in a sentence.

1. hall, haul   We had to haul the piano down the hall to the music room.

2. ad, add   _____

3. chilly, chili   _____

4. band, banned   _____

5. allowed, aloud   _____

D. Write about a forest fire. Use as many of the pairs of homographs below as you can. The pairs need not be in the same sentence.

   blaze, blaze   bear, bear   bark, bark   wind, wind

_____

_____

_____

_____

_____

E. Add a prefix or a suffix to each numbered word. Form a new word that means the same as the definition given. Use the new word in a sentence.

-less	-ness	re-	pre-	-able	mis-

1. use, "of no use"   _That broken shoelace is useless to me._

2. shy, "state of being shy" _____

3. pay, "to pay before" _____

4. write, "to write again" _____

5. count, "to count wrongly" _____

6. read, "able to be read" _____

F. Below each sentence are three words. Circle the two words that can form a compound word to complete the sentence. Write the compound word.

1. The roof of the house looked silver in the _____.
   light   car   moon

2. Did you suffer _____ on your skiing trip?
   frost   crystal   bite

3. The _____ is an amazing part of the body.
   sight   ball   eye

4. The moon was at its highest point at _____ .
   night   summer   mid

5. Were you able to _____ the cause of the problem?
   pin   point   ball

G. Write all the contractions you know that include each word below. Then use one of the contractions you formed in a sentence about a game you like to play.

1. will _____

   Sentence: _____

2. is _____

   Sentence: _____

3. I _____

   Sentence: _____

Recognizing Sentences

> ■ A **sentence** is a group of words that expresses a complete thought.   EXAMPLE: Many readers like stories about dogs.

A. Some of the groups of words below are sentences, and some are not. Write S before each group that is a sentence.

_____ 1. One famous dog story.

_____ 2. First appeared in a well-known magazine.

_____ 3. You may have read this famous story.

_____ 4. A collie named Lassie, who was owned by a poor farmer in Yorkshire, England.

_____ 5. To make money for his family.

_____ 6. The farmer sold Lassie to a wealthy duke.

_____ 7. Lassie was loyal to her first master, however.

_____ 8. Taken far away from Yorkshire.

_____ 9. She found her way back to her first home.

_____ 10. The story became a book and then a movie.

_____ 11. Helped two child actors on their way to stardom.

_____ 12. The real-life Lassie was a dog named Toots.

_____ 13. Toots was the companion of Eric Knight, the author of the story.

_____ 14. Lived in Yorkshire as a boy, but in the United States as an adult.

_____ 15. Knight died before his story, "Lassie Come Home," became famous.

_____ 16. Was killed in World War II.

_____ 17. Toots died on Knight's farm two years later.

B. Write a sentence about one of your favourite books.

_____

Types of Sentences

> - A **declarative** sentence makes a statement.
>   EXAMPLE: The telephone is ringing.
> - An **interrogative** sentence asks a question.
>   EXAMPLE: Where are you going?

A. Write _declarative_ or _interrogative_ after each sentence in the conversation below.

1. When did you get those new rollerblades? _____

2. I bought them yesterday. _____

3. Don't you think rollerblading is dangerous? _____

4. It's not any more dangerous than skateboarding. _____

5. I would like to learn to rollerblade. _____

6. Will you teach me? _____

7. Do you have a pair of rollerblades? _____

8. No, but I will buy some tomorrow. _____

B. Pretend that you are talking to the inventor of a new way to travel over land, sea, or in the air. Write four questions you'd ask and the inventor's answers. Label each sentence _D_ for declarative or _I_ for interrogative.

1. _____ _____

2. _____ _____

3. _____ _____

4. _____ _____

5. _____ _____

6. _____ _____

7. _____ _____

8. _____ _____

> - An **imperative** sentence expresses a command or a request.
>   EXAMPLES: Answer the telephone. Please don't shout.
> - An **exclamatory** sentence expresses strong or sudden feeling.
>   EXAMPLES: What a great movie it was! They're off!

A. Write <u>imperative</u> or <u>exclamatory</u> after each sentence.

1. Listen to that strange noise. _____

2. What a weird sound that is! _____

3. Go see what's there. _____

4. Go yourself. _____

5. I'm too scared! _____

6. Then look out the window. _____

7. What a cute kitten that is! _____

8. We shouldn't be scared! _____

9. Go get the kitten. _____

10. Come with me. _____

11. Oh, look! _____

12. Count the rest of the kittens in the basket. _____

13. Read the note attached to the handle. _____

14. What a surprise we got! _____

B. Write about a time you or someone you know was frightened by something. Use at least one exclamatory sentence and one imperative sentence.

_____

_____

_____

_____

_____

Complete Subjects and Predicates

> - Every sentence has two main parts – a **complete subject** and a **complete predicate**.
> - The complete subject includes all the words that name the person, place, or thing about which something is said.
>   EXAMPLE: **My sister Sara** plays tennis.
> - The complete predicate includes all the words that tell what the subject is or does.
>   EXAMPLE: My sister Sara **plays tennis**.

A. Write S before each group of words that may be used as a complete subject. Write P before each group of words that may be used as a complete predicate.

_____ 1. the mayor of our town

_____ 2. has a large town square

_____ 3. celebrate the holidays with parades

_____ 4. an election every four years

_____ 5. a map with every street in town

_____ 6. were planning to build a new swimming pool

B. Complete each sentence by writing a subject or a predicate.

1. All our town council members _____ .

2. _____ met in an important meeting.

3. _____ explained the problem.

4. Every interested citizen _____.

5. Our town's first settlers _____.

6. _____ planted crops.

7. _____ has been abandoned for years.

8. _____ should be preserved.

9. Some people _____.

10. _____ will have to come to vote.

11. My entire family _____.

- The **simple subject** of a sentence is the main word in the complete subject.   EXAMPLE: My friends go mushroom hunting. The words My friends make up the complete subject. The word friends is the simple subject.
- If the subject is made up of just one word, that word is both the complete subject and the simple subject.

A. In each sentence below, draw a line between the subject and the predicate. Underline the complete subject. Circle the simple subject.

1. Freshly-picked (morels) /are delicious.

2. These mushrooms can be found only in the spring.

3. A rich soil is best for morels.

4. Grassy spots are good places to look.

5. The spring must not be dry or too cold.

6. Damp earth is a good sign that morels may be found.

7. A clear, sunny sky means good hunting.

8. We never know where we'll find morels.

9. Tall, wet grasses often hide them.

10. We must work fast.

11. These spongy little mushrooms do not last long.

12. You might like to join us sometime.

B. Write five sentences about an activity you enjoy. Draw a line between the subject and the predicate. Underline the complete subject. Circle the simple subject.

1. _____

2. _____

3. _____

4. _____

5. _____

> ■ The **simple predicate** of a sentence is a verb within the complete predicate. The verb is an action or being word.
>   EXAMPLE: The Netherlands attracts many tourists. The words attracts many tourists make up the complete predicate. The verb attracts is the simple predicate.
> ■ The simple predicate may be a one-word verb or a verb of more than one word.
>   EXAMPLES: Joan **likes** tulips. She **is planning** a garden.

A. In each sentence below, draw a line between the subject and the predicate. Underline the complete predicate twice. Circle the simple predicate.

1. Many tourists visit the Netherlands in April or May.

2. The beautiful tulip blooms reach their height of glory during these months.

3. Visitors will see flowers everywhere.

4. Joan is dreaming of a trip to the Netherlands someday.

5. She has seen colourful pictures of tulips in catalogues.

6. The catalogues show tulips of all colours in full bloom.

7. Joan is anxious to see the tulips herself.

8. Passing travellers often buy large bunches of flowers.

9. Every Dutch city has flowers in it.

10. Flower vases are found in the cars of some Dutch people.

B. Add a predicate for each subject below. Circle the simple predicate.

1. My neighbour's garden _____.

2. I_____.

3. All of the flowers _____.

C. Write four sentences about a city or a country that you would like to visit or have visited. Draw a line between the subject and the predicate. Underline the complete predicate twice. Circle the simple predicate.

1. _____

2. _____

3. _____

4. _____

Understood Subjects

> - The subject of an imperative sentence is always the person to whom the command or request is given **(You)**. The subject does not appear in the sentence. Therefore, it is called an **understood subject**.
>   EXAMPLES: **(You)** Keep off the grass. **(You)** Close the door, please.

A. On the line after each imperative sentence below, write the understood subject and the simple predicate.

1. Turn left at the next light.   (You) Turn

2. Now turn right on Elm Street.   _____

3. Park in front of the house.   _____

4. Don't block the driveway.   _____

5. Leave enough room for them to leave.   _____

6. Help me with the food, please.   _____

7. Hold the door open until I get out.   _____

8. Get the bag off the back seat.   _____

9. Lock the car door, please.   _____

10. Check to see that the lights are off.   _____

11. Knock harder on the door.   _____

12. Try ringing the doorbell.   _____

B. Write four imperative sentences about a game or other activity. After each sentence, write the understood subject.

1. _____

2. _____

3. _____

4. _____

Using Compound Subjects

> ■ Two sentences that have different subjects but the same predicate can be combined to make one sentence. The two subjects are joined by and. The subject of the new sentence is called a **compound subject**.   EXAMPLE: **Craig** likes tall tales. **Jack** likes tall tales. **Craig** and **Jack** like tall tales.

A. In each sentence below, underline the subject. If the subject is compound, write C before the sentence.

_____ 1. Girls and boys love to hear stories about Big Joe Mufferaw.

_____ 2. Stompin' Tom Connors wrote a song about him.

_____ 3. Ottawa and Montréal were part of Joe's territory.

_____ 4. His exploits were based on those of a real-life lumberjack, Joseph Montferrand.

_____ 5. Lumberjacks and storytellers liked to tell tall tales about Joe's great strength and gentleness.

B. Combine each pair of sentences below to make a sentence that has a compound subject. Underline the compound subject.

1. People in England are familiar with the legend of Robin Hood.
    People all over the world are familiar with the legend of Robin Hood.

    _____

2. Great bravery made Robin Hood famous. Unusual skills made Robin Hood famous.

    _____

3. Prince John really existed. King Richard really existed.

    _____

4. Maid Marian was Robin's faithful companion.
    Little John was Robin's faithful companion.

    _____

C. Write a sentence using Robin Hood and his merry men as the subject.

    _____

    _____

© 1997 Gage Educational Publishing Company

> ■ Two sentences that have the same subject but different predicates can be combined to make one sentence. The two predicates may be joined by <u>or</u>, <u>and</u>, or <u>but</u>. The predicate of the sentence is called a **compound predicate**.
>
> EXAMPLE: A newspaper **informs its readers**.
> A newspaper **entertains its readers**. A newspaper **informs and entertains its readers**.

A. In each sentence below, underline the predicate. If the predicate is compound, write <u>C</u> before the sentence.

_____ 1. Our class wrote and printed its own newspaper.

_____ 2. Leslie was named editor-in-chief.

_____ 3. She assigned the stories and approved the final copies.

_____ 4. Wong and several other students were reporters.

_____ 5. They either wrote the news stories or edited the stories.

_____ 6. Wong interviewed a new student and wrote up the interview.

B. Combine each pair of sentences below to make a sentence that has a compound predicate. Underline the compound predicate.

1. Jenny covered the baseball game. Jenny described the best plays.

_____

2. Sue and Kim wrote jokes. Sue and Kim made up puzzles.

_____

3. Luis corrected the news stories. Luis wrote headlines.

_____

4. Alex typed the newspaper. Alex couldn't print the newspaper.

_____

C. Imagine that you are Luis or Jenny. Write a sentence that has a compound predicate which could begin the story on the baseball game.

_____

_____

> - A **simple sentence** has one subject and one predicate.
>   EXAMPLE: Great musicians/often start young.
> - A **compound sentence** is made up of two simple sentences joined by connecting words such as <u>and</u>, <u>but</u>, and <u>or</u>. A comma is placed before the connecting word
>   EXAMPLE: Wolfgang Mozart <u>was born in 1756</u> **and** he <u>died in 1791.</u>

A. Draw a line between each subject and predicate. Write <u>S</u> before each simple sentence. Write <u>C</u> before each compound sentence.

_____ 1. My friends and I often listen to music.

_____ 2. Rock music is good, but I enjoy classical music too.

_____ 3. Many musicians experiment with different types of music and different instruments.

_____ 4. Sometimes, rock musicians use classical instruments, like violins, or orchestras may play popular songs.

B. Combine each pair of simple sentences below into a compound sentence.

1. When he was four, Mozart wrote his first sonata.
   At six, he began playing at royal courts.

   _____

   _____

2. Beethoven's father wanted him to be like Mozart.
   He made him practise for long hours.

   _____

   _____

3. Beethoven began playing in public at age seven. His father said he was five.

   _____

   _____

4. Beethoven was deaf. He wrote beautiful music.

   _____

   _____

Lesson 18

Correcting Run-on Sentences

- Two or more sentences that are run together without the correct punctuation are called a **run-on sentence**.
  - EXAMPLE: Animals that carry their young in the mother's pouch are called marsupials, they live mainly in Australia.
- Correct a run-on sentence by making separate sentences from its parts.
  - EXAMPLE: Animals that carry their young in the mother's pouch are called marsupials. They live mainly in Australia.

A. Separate the run-on sentences below. Write the last word of the first sentence. Place a period after the word. Then write the first word of the second sentence. Be sure to capitalize the word. One run-on sentence is made of three sentences.

1. There are over two hundred kinds of marsupials all live in North or South America or in Australia.

   1. _____ marsupials. _____
      _____ All _____

2. The kangaroo is the largest marsupial, the male red kangaroo may be more than two metres.

   2. _____
      _____

3. Wallabies are similar to kangaroos, they are smaller than kangaroos, some are the size of a rabbit.

   3. _____
      _____
      _____
      _____

4. Kangaroos and wallabies live only in Australia, their hind feet are larger than their front feet.

   4. _____
      _____

B. Correct the run-on sentences in the paragraph below. Use the proofreader's symbols as shown in parentheses. (The opossum is active at night, it plays dead if frightened.) There will be seven sentences.

Opossums are the only marsupials that live north of Mexico, they also live in Central and South America. Opossums are greyish white, they have a long snout, hairless ears, and a long, hairless tail. Opossums have fifty teeth, the opossum mother has from five to twenty babies, each baby is the size of a kidney bean.

22   © 1997 Gage Educational Publishing Company   Unit 2, Sentences

A. Label each sentence as follows: Write D in front of each declarative sentence. Write IN in front of each interrogative sentence. Write IM in front of each imperative sentence. Write E in front of each exclamatory sentence. Write X if the group of words is not a sentence.

_____ 1. Did you know that the first bicycle had no pedals?

_____ 2. Very tiring and could not be steered.

_____ 3. The rider pushed himself forward by walking.

_____ 4. Made the first bicycle with pedals in Scotland.

_____ 5. What a great improvement it was!

_____ 6. What did the public think of this bicycle?

_____ 7. Get that machine off the road.

_____ 8. Say today about bicycles?

_____ 9. They're one of the best inventions ever.

_____ 10. Tell me what you think.

_____ 11. I love riding mine!

_____ 12. Maybe we can ride together sometime

B. In each sentence below, draw a line between the complete subject and the complete predicate. Underline the simple subject once. Underline the simple predicate twice. One sentence has an understood subject. Write the understood subject on the line after that sentence.

1. The next bicycle was known as the "boneshaker." _____

2. Its wheels were made of wood. _____

3. A new feature was iron tires. _____

4. Guess how this bicycle got its name. _____

5. Wire-spoked wheels came next. _____

6. The front wheel gradually increased in size. _____

7. The rear wheel became smaller. _____

8. They began using iron instead of wood for parts. _____

9. An air-filled rubber tire brought comfort. _____

10. More people turned to bicycling for enjoyment. _____

C. Label the sentences below as follows: SS if the sentence has a simple subject; SP if the sentence has a simple predicate; CS if the sentence has a compound subject; and CP if the sentence has a compound predicate.

_____ _____ 1. Water is necessary to all life on Earth.

_____ _____ 2. Plants and animals need water to live.

_____ _____ 3. Living things would weaken and die without it.

_____ _____ 4. Some plants and animals eat and breathe underwater.

_____ _____ 5. Other animals live on land and play in water.

D. Underline each compound subject once and each compound predicate twice. Circle each simple subject and simple predicate.

1. Rain and sleet are two forms that water can take.

2. Water also becomes snow and hail.

3. Wind tosses and swirls snowflakes into drifts.

4. Sunshine heats and evaporates water.

E. Write simple or compound before each sentence.

_____ 1. It was time to leave.

_____ 2. We were taking a trip, so we got up early.

_____ 3. The sun was not up yet, and there was a chill in the air.

_____ 4. We got into the car, and I turned on the heat.

_____ 5. The sunrise was quite beautiful, and we were glad we saw it.

F. Rewrite the paragraph. Combine simple sentences into compound sentences, and separate run-on sentences.

It was hot in the car, we rolled down the windows. The air was fresh. It felt cool on our faces. Larry began to sing he sang off-key. The song was funny. The song was one we all knew. Soon we were all singing, we sounded terrible, we had fun anyway.

_____

_____

_____

_____

A. Two of the groups of words below are sentences, and three are not. Write S before each sentence. Add whatever is needed to the groups of words to make them complete sentences.

_____ 1. The minute Scott heard his name called. _____

_____ 2. Amy was sure that her name would be called next. _____

_____ 3. The feeling of nervousness was mounting. _____

_____ 4. Only three possible names. _____

_____ 5. Amy could hardly. _____

B. Complete each sentence below to make the kind of sentence named.

Declarative   1. An expert is one who _____

Interrogative   2. Why did the expert _____

Imperative   3. Read the _____

Exclamatory   4. What a perfect _____

C. Add to each subject or predicate below whatever is needed to make a sentence. Underline the simple subject once and the simple predicate twice.

1. The dangerous tornado _____.

2. A raging wind storm _____.

3. _____ had flooded the downtown area.

4. Homeowners for several blocks _____.

5. _____ created puddles two feet deep.

6. _____ rescued a helpless motorist.

D. Write three sentences in which You is the understood subject. Include one of the verbs below in each sentence.

hide	do	think	give	walk	sit

1. _____

2. _____

3 _____

E. Write a compound subject for each predicate. Underline the simple predicate twice.

1. _____ opened the special event.

2. _____ were given to the school.

3. _____ presented the awards.

4. _____ received a lot of praise.

F. Write a compound predicate for each subject. Underline the simple subject.

1. The bank robber _____

2. The undercover detective _____

3. One innocent bystander _____

4. The trembling bank clerk _____

G. Rewrite the sentences below by making one of these improvements: (a) combine sentences by using compound subjects or compound predicates; (b) combine simple sentences to make compound sentences; (c) correct run-on sentences.

1. Alex and Steve were writing a play, they wrote together often.

    _____

2. This time they couldn't agree. They argued for hours.

    _____

3. Alex would say one thing. Steve would say the opposite.

    _____

4. They were both right. They were both wrong. Neither would give in.

    _____

5. Finally, Alex stood up, he said he was leaving.

    _____

6. Steve couldn't believe it. He couldn't believe that their argument had caused such a serious problem.

    _____

7. They glared at each other, they started laughing.

    _____

8. They decided to forget the problem. They decided to work together as a team.

    _____

Lesson 19 Nouns

> - A **noun** is a word that names a person, place, thing, or quality.
>
>   EXAMPLES: Rachel, Chad, city, Alberta, shell, animal, love, freedom, happiness

A. Write nouns that name the following:

1. Four people you admire

   _____   _____

   _____   _____

2. Four places you would like to visit

   _____   _____

   _____   _____

3. Six things you use every day

   _____   _____

   _____   _____

4. Four qualities you would like to have

   _____   _____

   _____   _____

5. Four provinces in Canada

   _____   _____

   _____   _____

B. Find and underline twenty-four nouns in the sentences below.

1. Every region of Canada has attractions for tourists.
2. British Columbia has stunning views of the mountains and the ocean.
3. The area around Banff, Alberta is rugged and beautiful.
4. The broad fields of wheat on the Prairies can take your breath away.
5. Montréal and Toronto are the most exciting cities in the country.
6. The eastern provinces are proud of their picturesque fishing villages.
7. The untouched beauty of the North draws people back again and again.

- There are two main classes of nouns: **common** and **proper nouns**.
- A **common noun** is a word that names any one of a class of objects.   EXAMPLES: girl, city, dog
- A **proper noun** is the name of a particular person, place, or thing. It begins with a capital letter.
    EXAMPLES: Sue, Africa, Digger

A. Write a proper noun for each common noun below.

1. city _____
2. school _____
3. friend _____
4. ocean _____
5. province _____
6. car _____
7. singer _____
8. day _____
9. lake _____

10. street _____
11. game _____
12. river _____
13. woman _____
14. country _____
15. man _____
16. prime minister _____
17. month _____
18. planet _____

B. Write a common noun for each proper noun below.

1. Ontario _____
2. November _____
3. Thanksgiving _____
4. Beth _____
5. December _____
6. Jamaica _____
7. *Call of the Wild* _____
8. Saturday _____
9. Alaska _____

10. South America _____
11. Dr. Cooke _____
12. Rocky Mountains _____
13. Pierre Trudeau _____
14. Sahara _____
15. Vancouver _____
16. Mexico _____
17. Saturn _____
18. Jason _____

Lesson 21

Singular and Plural Nouns

- A **singular noun** is a noun that names one person, place, or thing.   EXAMPLES: knife, church, boy, mouse
- A **plural noun** is a noun that names more than one person, place, or thing.   EXAMPLES: knives, churches, boys, mice

---

A. Write S before each singular noun below. Then write its plural form. Write P before each plural noun. Then write its singular form. You may wish to check the spellings in a dictionary.

_____ 1. boots _____

_____ 2. army _____

_____ 3. match _____

_____ 4. maps _____

_____ 5. punches _____

_____ 6. foot _____

_____ 7. hero _____

_____ 8. alley _____

_____ 9. baby _____

_____ 10. women _____

_____ 11. halves _____

_____ 12. skies _____

_____ 13. wife _____

_____ 14. boxes _____

_____ 15. beach _____

_____ 16. book _____

B. Write the plural form of each word below to complete the sentences.

watch	shelf	child	story	monkey	player

1. There are many interesting _____ in that magazine.

2. The cover story on timepieces describes the making of _____.

3. A sports story contains conversations with three of the nation's leading

   football _____ .

4. A do-it-yourself article shows how to build _____ that will hold an aquarium.

5. Unusual _____ and apes are shown in a picture story.

6. This month's special article is a selection of poems and stories by

   German _____ .

Singular Possessive Nouns

> - A **possessive noun shows** possession of the noun that follows.   EXAMPLES: mother's car, the dog's bone
> - To form the possessive of most singular nouns, add an apostrophe (') and -s.   EXAMPLES: Sally's room, the city's mayor

A. Write the possessive form of the noun in parentheses to complete each phrase.

1. the _____ leash (dog)

2. the _____ lawn (neighbour)

3. one of the _____ engines (plane)

4. _____ greatest ambition (Ann)

5. to _____ house (grandmother)

6. the _____ paw (tiger)

7. my _____ farm (sister)

8. your _____ best friend (brother)

9. our _____ advice (mother)

10. the _____ gym (school)

11. my _____ apple (teacher)

12. that _____ fur (cat)

13. the _____ teeth (dinosaur)

14. the _____ coach (team)

B. Write each of the phrases below in a shorter way.

1. the friend of Amanda _____ Amanda's friend _____

2. the car of the friend _____

3. the keeper of the zoo _____

4. the roar of the lion _____

5. the cage of the tiger _____

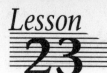

Plural Possessive Nouns

> - To form the possessive of a plural noun ending in -s, add only an apostrophe.
>   EXAMPLES: the boys' coats, the books' covers
> - To form the possessive of a plural noun that does not end in -s, add an apostrophe and -s.
>   EXAMPLES: men's suits, children's toys

A. Complete the chart below. You may wish to check the spellings in a dictionary.

Singular noun	Plural noun	Singular possessive	Plural possessive
1. horse	horses	horse's	horses'
2. bird			
3. teacher			
4. child			
5. truck			
6. doctor			
7. man			
8. church			

B. Rewrite each sentence using a possessive noun.

1. The cat of the Smiths has three kittens.

_____

2. The names of the kittens are Frisky, Midnight, and Puff.

_____

3. The dogs of the neighbours are very playful.

_____

4. The pen of the dogs is in the yard.

_____

5. The curiosity of the cats might get them into trouble.

_____

> - A **verb** is a word that shows action. The verb may show action that can be seen.
>   EXAMPLE: Jane **opened** the door.
> - The verb may show action that cannot be seen.
>   EXAMPLE: Mary **thought** about it.

A. Underline the verb in each sentence.

1. Several years ago people <u>started</u> recycling materials.
2. Today people recycle many things.
3. They buy special containers to sort their wastes.
4. In years past, few people recycled.
5. People threw most of their garbage away.
6. Some people burned their garbage.
7. This harmed the environment.
8. Then groups of people asked companies to recycle used materials.
9. Today many companies recycle materials.
10. People throw less garbage away.
11. Many groups work hard to encourage recycling.
12. Responsible companies now recycle many things.

**B. Complete each sentence with one of the verbs below.
Use each verb once.**

believe	felt	hoped	knew	remember	studied	thought	worried

1. Yoko really _____ about the math test.

2. She _____ every day.

3. She _____ she could pass the test.

4. During the test, Yoko _____ carefully about each problem.

5. Could she _____ all she had studied?

6. She _____ more confident once the test was over.

7. She _____ that she had done well.

8. When Yoko got her test back, she couldn't _____ she got an A!

Lesson 25

Helping Verbs

> ■ A verb may have a **main verb** and one or more **helping verbs**. Such a verb is called a **verb phrase**.
>
> EXAMPLES: The bells **were ringing**. Where **have** you **been hiding**?

A. Underline each main verb. Circle each helping verb. Some verbs do not have a helping verb.

1. (Have) you <u>heard</u> of Karen Kain?

2. She was born in 1951 in Hamilton, Ontario.

3. The National Ballet of Canada had been founded that same year.

4. Karen was taken to see *Giselle* when she was eight.

5. She had always been interested in dance.

6. After *Giselle*, she wanted to be a dancer.

7. In 1962 she was accepted at the National Ballet School.

8. The years of training would be hard on Karen.

9. She was always afraid of being thrown out.

10. But Karen would never abandon her dream.

11. In 1969, she was asked to join the National Ballet.

12. She was soon a principal ballerina.

13. Karen has had an extraordinary career.

14. She has danced with Rudolph Nureyev.

15. All her hard work has paid off.

B. Complete each sentence by adding <u>have</u>, <u>will</u>, or <u>would</u>.

1. Maria and Hutoshi _____ like to go swimming.

2. They _____ received permission from their parents.

3. This _____ be their second trip to the pool today.

Lesson
26
Present and Past Tense

- A verb in the **present tense** shows an action that happens now.   EXAMPLE: I **watch** TV.
- A verb in the **past tense** shows an action that happened in the past.   EXAMPLE: I **watched** TV.

A. Underline each verb in the present tense.

1. Electricity causes lightning.
2. One bolt discharges millions of volts.
3. Lightning always follows the easiest path.
4. Lightning rods carry lightning safely to the ground.
5. Thunder often accompanies lightning.
6. No one exactly understands their relationship.
7. Thunderstorms never occur in polar regions.
8. They happen almost every day on the island of Java.

B. Underline each verb or verb phrase in the past tense.

1. One man had been in an accident.
2. He was blind and couldn't hear very well.
3. Nine years later, lightning struck him.
4. Suddenly, he could see again!
5. His hearing had also returned.
6. Hair grew on his bald head.
7. Scientists couldn't explain it.

C. List four verbs you know.

present tense	past tense
1.	
2.	
3.	
4.	

      Unit 3, Grammar and Usage

Lesson 27 — Future Tense

> ■ A verb in the **future tense** shows an action that will happen
> at some time in the future. The helping verb <u>will</u> is used
> with the present tense form of the verb.
>   EXAMPLE: I **will meet** you tomorrow.

A. Write a verb in the future tense to complete each sentence.

1. Sue _____ the invitations.

2. David and Andrew _____ what games to play.

3. We all _____ the balloons with air.

4. Mary and Ella _____ the table decorations.

5. Rashid and Rosa _____ the cake.

6. Chris _____ of a way to get Tony to come over.

7. We all _____ in the back room.

8. When Chris and Tony come in, everyone _____ , "Surprise!"

**B. The sentences below show an event that happened in the past. Rewrite
each underlined verb to change the event to a time in the future.**

1. Carla <u>sent</u> a letter to the Round-the-World Travel Agency. _____will send_____

2. She <u>received</u> an answer in a day or two. _____

3. The agency <u>mailed</u> her folders containing information
   about exciting places to visit. _____

4. Carla <u>studied</u> the information. _____

5. She <u>chose</u> to write about three places. _____

6. Then she <u>planned</u> an imaginary trip to those three
   places. _____

7. She <u>wrote</u> in detail about her imaginary trip. _____

8. She <u>designed</u> her report with pictures from the
   travel agency folders. _____

9. She <u>made</u> an interesting cover for her report. _____

10. Then she <u>hoped</u> for a good grade. _____

Lesson 28

Subject-Verb Agreement

- A **singular subject** must have a **singular verb**.
  EXAMPLES: Jane **lives** there. She **does walk** to school. She **doesn't live** near me.
- A **plural subject** must have a **plural verb**.
  EXAMPLES: Jane and her sister **live** there. They **do walk** to school. They **don't live** near me.
- <u>You</u> and <u>I</u> must have a plural verb.

- **Write S over each singular subject. Write P over each plural subject. Then underline the correct verb in parentheses.**

1. Many stories (tell, tells) how dogs become friends of people.

2. A story by Rudyard Kipling (say, says) that Wild Dog agreed to help hunt and guard in exchange for bones.

3. After that, Wild Dog (become, becomes) First Friend.

4. Many dogs never (leave, leaves) their masters.

5. In another story, a dog (doesn't, don't) leave his master's dead body and dies in the Arctic cold.

6. There are few people in history that (doesn't, don't) record the usefulness of dogs.

7. Diggings in Egypt (prove, proves) that the dog was a companion in ancient Egypt.

8. Bones of dogs (does, do) appear in Egyptian graves.

9. Ancient Greek vases (picture, pictures) dogs on them.

10. Today the Canine Vision organization (train, trains) dogs to guide people who can't see.

11. One man who can't see said, "My eyes (have, has) a wet nose."

12. A dog (does, do) have excellent hearing and smelling abilities.

13. What person (doesn't, don't) agree that a dog is a person's best friend?

---

36   © 1997 Gage Educational Publishing Company   **Unit 3, Grammar and Usage**

> - A **linking verb** is a verb that joins the subject of a sentence with a word in the predicate.
>   EXAMPLES: Bob **is** an artist. Bob **was** late.
> - A singular subject must have a singular linking verb.
>   EXAMPLES: Maria **is** a singer. Maria **was** happy.
> - A plural subject must have a plural linking verb.
>   EXAMPLES: Becky and Lynn **are** sisters. The sisters **were** happy.
> - You must have a plural linking verb.

A. Write S over each singular subject. Write P over each plural subject. Then circle the correct linking verb.

1. Tracy (is, are) a clown.

2. Her brothers (is, are) acrobats.

3. Tracy and her brothers (was, were) in a show.

4. Tracy (was, were) funny.

5. Her brothers (was, were) daring.

6. The people watching (was, were) delighted.

7. Tracy (was, were) amusing with her big red nose.

8. Tracy's brothers (was, were) high in the air on a swing.

9. (Was, Were) you at their show?

10. Tracy (is, are) glad that I went to see her perform.

B. Circle the correct linking verb in parentheses.

1. Ice skating (is, are) a popular winter sport today.

2. (Isn't, Aren't) there a skating rink or pond in every northern town?

3. In our town, there (is, are) an indoor rink.

4. The discovery of ice skating (were, was) an accident.

5. An Arctic settler who slipped on a piece of bone and skidded across the ice (was, were) the inventor of the ice skate.

6. Pieces of bone attached to his feet (was, were) the first ice skates.

7. Now we (is, are) all able to enjoy his invention.

8. That (was, were) a lucky day for all ice skaters!

- Never use a helping verb with <u>went</u>, <u>did</u>, <u>saw</u>, or <u>sang</u>.
  EXAMPLES: Sue **did** her work. Sam **went** home. Sarah **sang** a song.
- Always use a helping verb with <u>gone</u>, <u>done</u>, <u>seen</u>, or <u>sung</u>.
  EXAMPLES: Sarah **has done** her work. Mary **had** not **seen** me.

A. Circle the correct verb in parentheses.

1. The class members (did, done) very well on their music project.
2. Most of them had (gone, went) to extra practices.
3. They (sang, sung) at the special spring concert.
4. The class had (sang, sung) in the concert before, but they (did, done) even better this year.
5. The teacher said she had never (saw, seen) a class work so well together.
6. The teacher said they had (sang, sung) beautifully.
7. They (sang, sung) so well that she was very proud of them.
8. The week after the concert, the class (gone, went) to a music museum.
9. The trip was a reward because the class had (did, done) so well.
10. The class (saw, seen) pictures of famous musicians at the museum.
11. After they had (saw, seen) an exhibit of unusual music boxes, they wished the boxes were for sale.
12. What do you think the teacher (did, done)?
13. She took the class to a music shop she had (gone, went) to before.
14. The teacher and the shop owner had (sang, sung) together.
15. They had (gone, went) to the same music school.
16. So the class (went, gone) to this shop and saw many little musical toys.
17. In the shop they (saw, seen) many small music boxes.

B. Write the correct form of each verb in parentheses.

1. (go)   Kate has _____ to voice class.
2. (do)   She has _____ that every day for a year.
3. (see)   Her friends have _____ her sing in public.
4. (sing)   She _____ last week at the auditorium.

Lesson 31

Forms of *Break, Drink, Take,* and *Write*

> - Never use a helping verb with <u>broke</u>, <u>drank</u>, <u>took</u>, or <u>wrote</u>.
>   EXAMPLES: Kim **broke** her arm. Jack **wrote** a letter.
> - Always use a helping verb with <u>broken</u>, <u>drunk</u>, <u>taken</u>, or <u>written</u>.
>   EXAMPLES: Kim **has broken** her arm. Jack **had written** a note.

A. Complete each sentence with the correct form of one of the verbs below.

broke, broken	drank, drunk	took, taken	wrote, written

1. Rick _____ his time writing the letter.

2. He had _____ Janet's sculpture from her, and he needed to

   apologize.

3. He _____ slowly and carefully, thinking hard about each word.

4. Whenever he paused, he _____ water from the glass on

   his desk.

5. In the letter, he said he was sorry he had _____ the sculpture.

6. Although he tried to be careful, he _____ it.

7. He _____ that he would never do anything like that again.

8. Then he read what he had _____ .

9. He saw that he had _____ all of his water.

10. It had _____ all his courage to write that letter.

B. Write the correct form of each verb in parentheses.

1. (take) Alan had _____ his dog for a long walk and was thirsty.

2. (drink) So he had _____ a glass of fruit juice.

3. (break) He was careful and had not _____ the glass.

4. (break) But then his dog, Ruby, had _____ it.

5. (write) Now Alan has _____ a note of apology.

Unit 3, Grammar and Usage   © 1997 Gage Educational Publishing Company   **39**

- Never use a helping verb with <u>ate</u>, <u>drew</u>, <u>gave</u>, or <u>rang</u>.
  EXAMPLES: Ann **ate** her lunch. The telephone **rang**.
- Always use a helping verb with <u>eaten</u>, <u>drawn</u>, <u>given</u>, or <u>rung</u>.
  EXAMPLES: Ann **has eaten** her lunch. The telephone **has rung**.

A. Complete each sentence with the correct form of the verb in parentheses.

1. (give) Martha _____ samples of the granola bars she had made to three of her friends.

2. (eat) The bars were soon _____ , and there were cries of "More!"

3. (eat) "You _____ those already?" Martha asked.

4. (give) "I should have _____ you the recipe."

5. (eat) "Please do!" said her friends. "We have never _____ anything so delicious."

6. (give) "I _____ them to you for your health's sake," said Martha.

7. (ring) Just then the telephone _____ .

8. (draw) "Hello," said Martha. "You have _____ my name?"

9. (draw) "They _____ my name as the winner!" she told her friends.

10. (ring) "If that phone hadn't _____ when it did, we would have gone home," said Paul.

11. (eat) "If you had _____ any faster, you would have missed all the excitement," said Martha.

B. Circle the correct verb in parentheses.

1. The telephone has just (rang, rung).

2. Pauline and Betty have (eat, eaten) breakfast and are looking for something to do.

3. Now Joseph has (gave, given) them a call to ask if they would like to come to his house.

Lesson 33 — Forms of *Begin, Fall, Steal,* and *Throw*

> - Never use a helping verb with <u>began</u>, <u>fell</u>, <u>stole</u>, or <u>threw</u>.
>   EXAMPLES: Sue **began** to run. Jose **fell** down.
> - Always use a helping verb with <u>begun</u>, <u>fallen</u>, <u>stolen</u>, or <u>thrown</u>.
>   EXAMPLES: Sue **had begun** to run. Jose **had fallen**.

A. Circle the correct verb in parentheses.

1. Spring baseball practice had just (began, begun).

2. The pitchers on the Blasters' team had (threw, thrown) a few balls.

3. The other Blasters (began, begun) to practise.

4. They would need much practice, because they had (fell, fallen) into last place at the end of last season.

5. The Blasters' coaches (threw, thrown) themselves into their work.

6. The biggest job (fell, fallen) on the batting and base-running coach.

7. The team batting average had (fell, fallen) out of sight.

8. And the players had (stole, stolen) only forty bases last year.

9. The coach said, "Our team motto will be 'We have just (began, begun) to fight!' "

10. With that, the Blasters (fell, fallen) to work.

11. The pitchers (threw, thrown) many different kinds of pitches.

12. The fastest pitch was (threw, thrown) at 120 km/h.

13. The batters were hitting everything that was (threw, thrown) to them.

B. Write the correct form of each verb in parentheses.

1. (steal)   In last night's opening game, Nick, our team's fastest

    base runner, had _____ home.

2. (begin) We had _____ to warm up Willis, our relief pitcher,

    before the sixth inning.

3. (throw) He had _____ the ball so well last year that

    no batters could hit his pitches.

4. (begin) After Willis won last night's game for us, we told him that

    he had _____ our season in great style.

Subject and Object Pronouns

- A **pronoun** is a word that is used in place of a noun.
  EXAMPLES: Eli read a story. **He** enjoyed the story.
- A **subject pronoun** is a pronoun that is used as the subject of a sentence. He, I, it, she, they, we, and you are subject pronouns.
  EXAMPLES: **She** helped Joe. **I** helped, too.
- An **object pronoun** is a pronoun that is used in place of a noun that receives the action of the verb. Her, him, it, me, them, us, and you are object pronouns.
  EXAMPLES: Diane called **me**. I answered **her**.

A. Circle the subject pronoun that could be used in place of the underlined subject.

1. Susan (Her, She) saw the bus nearing the corner.
2. Joseph (Him, He) ran down the street to stop the bus.
3. The children (Them, They) saw Susan from the bus windows.
4. Ann (Her, She) called to Ms. Thomas, the driver, to wait.
5. The bus (It, He) stopped just in time.
6. Ms. Thomas (Her, She) let Susan on the bus.
7. Then Susan (her, she) waved goodbye to Joseph.
8. Susan (Her, She) was glad the bus had waited for her.

B. Circle the correct object pronoun that could be used in place of the underlined object.

1. "Tony invited Bill and (I, me) to his birthday party," said Tom.
2. "He asked Tom and Bill (us, we) to be right on time," Bill said.
3. "Tony's friends are giving Tony (he, him) a special gift," Tom said. "They are giving him tickets to the baseball game."
4. "They bought the tickets (them, they) last week."
5. Bill asked, "Do you think Tony's friends bought Tony, Bill, and Tom (us, we) front row seats?"
6. "Let's ask Tony's friends (them, they)," Tom answered.

Lesson 35

Possessive Pronouns

> - A **possessive pronoun** is a pronoun that shows who or what owns something.
>   EXAMPLES: The shoes are **mine**. Those are **my** shoes.
> - The possessive pronouns <u>hers</u>, <u>mine</u>, <u>ours</u>, <u>theirs</u>, and <u>yours</u> stand alone.
>   EXAMPLES: The dog is **mine**. This book is **yours**.
> - The possessive pronouns <u>her</u>, <u>its</u>, <u>my</u>, <u>our</u>, <u>their</u>, and <u>your</u> must be used before nouns.
>   EXAMPLES: **Their** house is grey. **Her** cat is white.
> - The pronoun <u>his</u> may be used either way.
>   EXAMPLES: That is **his** car. The car is **his**.

A. Circle the possessive pronoun that completes each sentence.

1. Carol lent me (her, hers) sweater.

2. I thought that (her, hers) was warmer than mine.

3. We often trade (our, ours) jackets and sweaters.

4. I hope I don't forget which are (her, hers) and which are (my, mine).

5. My cousin Patty and I have the same problem with (our, ours) bikes.

6. Both of (our, ours) are the same make and model.

7. The only difference is that (mine, my) handlebar grips are blue and (her, hers) are green.

8. What kind of dog is (your, yours)?

9. (Your, Yours) dog's ears are pointed.

10. (It, Its) tail is stubby.

B. Complete each pair of sentences by writing the correct possessive pronoun.

1. Bill owns a beautiful horse named Tony.

    _____ spots are brown and white.

2. Bill has taught the horse some tricks.

    In fact, _____ horse counts with its hoof.

3. Bill's sisters have horses, too.

    Bill is going to train them for _____ sisters.

Lesson 36

Adjectives

> - An **adjective** is a word that describes a noun or a pronoun.
>   EXAMPLE: The field is dotted with **beautiful** flowers.
> - Adjectives usually tell **what kind**, **which one**, or **how many**.
>   EXAMPLES: **tall** trees, the **other** hat, **five** dollars

A. In the sentences below, underline each adjective and circle the noun it describes. Some sentences may contain more than one adjective. Do not include a, an, or the.

1. The early Greeks thought a healthy body was important.
2. They believed that strong bodies meant healthy minds.
3. The Olympics began in Greece in the distant past.
4. The great god Zeus and the powerful Cronus both wanted to own Earth.
5. They battled on the high peaks of the beautiful mountains of Greece.
6. Zeus won the mighty struggle, and the first Olympics were

   held in the peaceful valley below Mount Olympus.

B. Expand the meaning of each sentence below by writing an adjective to describe each underlined noun.

1. The _____ runners from _____ nations lined up
   for the race.

2. Several _____ skaters competed for the _____ medal.

3. The _____ skiers sped down the _____ slopes.

4. We noticed the _____ colours of their _____ clothing

   against the _____ snow.

5. Hundreds of _____ fans greeted the _____ winners
   of each event.

6. As the _____ song of the winner's country

   was played, _____ tears streamed down her _____ face.

C. Fill in each blank with an adjective telling how many or which one.

1. _____ days of vacation   3. the _____ row of desks

2. the _____ race   4. _____ library books

Adjectives That Compare

> - Adjectives that compare two nouns end in -er.
>   EXAMPLES: Jack is **taller** than Bill. Bill is **heavier** than Jack.
> - Adjectives that compare more than two nouns end in -est.
>   EXAMPLE: Sam is the **tallest** and **heaviest** in the class.
> - Most longer adjectives use more and most to compare.
>   EXAMPLES: **more** beautiful, **most** beautiful

- **Underline the correct form of the adjective.**

1. Last year's science fair was the (bigger, biggest) one we have ever had.

2. For one thing, it had the (larger, largest) attendance ever.

3. Also, most students felt that the projects were (more interesting, most interesting) than last year's.

4. Of the two models of the solar system, Ray's was the (larger, largest).

5. However, Mary's model was (more accurate, most accurate) in scale.

6. The judges had a difficult task, but they gave the (higher, highest) rating to Mary's model.

7. Sue's, Tim's, and Becky's projects on cameras drew the (bigger, biggest) crowds at the fair.

8. These projects were the (more popular, most popular) of all.

9. Sue's project had the (prettier, prettiest) display of photographs.

10. But Becky's showed the (greater, greatest) understanding of a camera's workings.

11. Tim's project, however, was the (finer, finest) all-around project of the three.

12. One judge said, "This was the (harder, hardest) job I've ever had."

- An **adverb** is a word that describes a verb. It tells **how**, **when**, **where**, or **how often** the action shown by a verb happens.
- Many adverbs end in -ly.
  - EXAMPLES: The bell rang **loudly**. The bell rang **today**.
    The bell rang **downstairs**. The bell rang **often**.

A. Circle each verb. Then underline each adverb that describes the verb. Next, write <u>how</u>, <u>when</u>, <u>where</u>, or <u>how often</u>.

1. Rob and Jeff (had talked) daily about visiting the empty   how often
   old house.

2. They often walked by it on their way to school.   _____

3. But they seldom had time to stop.   _____

4. They suddenly decided that today was the day.   _____

5. So on the way home from school, they slipped
   quietly through the front gate.   _____

6. They crept carefully up the creaky front steps.   _____

7. Rob quietly opened the front door.   _____

8. Jeff then peered into the darkness of the front hall.   _____

9. A draft of wind instantly swept through the house.   _____

10. The back door banged loudly.   _____

11. Rob and Jeff ran swiftly out the front door and
    through the gate.   _____

12. They never returned to that empty old house.   _____

B. Choose the correct adverb for each sentence.

finally	late	nervously	Suddenly

1. Dean's plane was arriving _____ .

2. Nancy kept glancing _____ at the clock in the airport.

3. _____ the gate lights flashed.

4. Dean's plane _____ had landed.

Adverbs That Compare

> ■ Add -er when using short adverbs to compare two actions.
>   EXAMPLE: Joe ran **faster** than Jill.
> ■ Add -est when using short adverbs to compare more than two actions.
>   EXAMPLE: Jim ran **fastest** of all.
> ■ Use more or most with longer adverbs and with adverbs that end in -ly when comparing two or more than two actions.
>   EXAMPLES: Rob answered **more quickly** than Sue. Tim answered **most quickly** of all.

■ **Complete each sentence below by writing the correct form of the adverb shown in parentheses.**

1. (close)   Amy lives _____ to Lake Hope than we do.

2. (early)   She usually arrives there _____ than we do.

3. (fast)   Amy says that I can row _____ than anyone

    else on the lake.

4. (quickly)   But my cousin Jake can bait a hook _____

    than I can.

5. (patiently) Amy can wait _____ than Jake

    and I put together.

6. (carefully) Jake and I are both careful, but Amy baits

    the hook _____ .

7. (quietly)   Jake and I try to see who can sit _____ .

8. (soon)   I usually break the silence _____ than Jake.

9. (skilfully) I'd have to admit that Amy fishes _____

    of the three of us.

10. (happily)   And no one I know welcomes us to her

    home _____ than she does.

> - Remember that adjectives describe nouns or pronouns.
>   Adjectives tell **what kind**, **which one**, or **how many**.
>   EXAMPLES: **blue** sky, **this** year, **several** pages
> - Remember that adverbs describe verbs. Adverbs tell **how**,
>   **when**, **where**, or **how often**.
>   EXAMPLES: Walk **slowly**. Go **now**. Come **here**.

- **In the sentences below, underline each adjective. Circle each adverb.**

   1. Three men were given licences to hunt once on a rugged Kodiak island.

   2. They had finally received permission to hunt the wild
      animals that live there.

   3. Their purpose was different than the word "hunt" usually suggests.

   4. The men were zoo hunters and would try to catch
      three bear cubs.

   5. They confidently expected to take the young cubs to a
      new home at a distant zoo.

   6. Once on the hilly island, the hopeful men quietly
      unpacked and then lay down for six hours of rest.

   7. The next day, the men carefully scanned the rocky cliffs
      through powerful glasses.

   8. They saw a huge brown bear with three cubs
      tumbling playfully around her.

   9. The men spent two hours climbing quietly up to a point
      overlooking that ledge.

  10. A large den could barely be seen in the rocks.

  11. The wily hunters knew that bears never charge uphill.

  12. However, the human scent immediately warned the watchful
      mother bear.

  13. With a fierce roar, she walked heavily out of the cave
      and stared up at the men with her beady eyes.

  14. One of the men tightly tied a red bandana and a dirty
      sock to a rope and threw the bundle down the slope.

  15. The curious bear charged clumsily after it.

  16. Quickly the men dropped to the wide ledge below.

  17. But the wise cubs successfully hid from the men.

- A **preposition** is a word that shows the relationship of a noun or a pronoun to another word in the sentence.
  - EXAMPLES: The cat **under** the tree is mine.
- Some prepositions include: in, down, to, by, of, with, for, and at.
- A **prepositional phrase** is a group of words that begins with a preposition and ends with a noun or a pronoun.
  - EXAMPLES: **in** the house, **down** the street, **to** us

A. Underline the prepositional phrase in each sentence below. Circle the prepositions.

1. The box (on) the dining room table was wrapped.

2. A friend of Marta's was having a birthday.

3. Marta had been saving money for weeks so she could buy the present.

4. Now Marta was dressing in her bedroom.

5. Marta's little sister Tina toddled into the dining room.

6. She pulled the tablecloth, and the box fell to the floor.

7. Marta heard a thump and ran to the dining room.

8. Tina hid under the table.

9. The playful look on her face made Marta smile.

B. Underline ten prepositional phrases in the paragraph below.

When I went into the store, I looked at coats. I needed a new one to wear during the winter. I left my old one on the bus. When I got on the bus, I noticed it was very hot. I took off my coat and put it under my seat. When I got off the bus, I forgot it. When I asked about it, I was told to look at the office. It was not there.

C. Give directions for a treasure hunt. Use the prepositional phrases below in your sentences.

around the corner	near the school	under a rock	beneath the tree

_____

_____

_____

_____

- <u>May</u> expresses **permission**.
  - EXAMPLE: **May** I go to town?
- <u>Can</u> expresses the **ability** to do something.
  - EXAMPLE: She **can** play well.
- <u>Good</u> is an adjective. It tells **what kind**.
  - EXAMPLE: My sister is a **good** cook.
- <u>Well</u> is an adverb. It tells **how**.
  - EXAMPLE: Did you do **well** today?

■ **Underline the correct word in each sentence below.**

1. (Can, May) I use the pen on your desk, Sam?
2. Yes, you (can, may) use it, but I doubt that you (can, may) make it work, Sara.
3. Look, Sam! It's working (good, well) now.
4. That's (good, well). How did you make it work?
5. (Can, May) we have an early appointment, Doctor Morris?
6. Just a moment. I'll see whether I (can, may) arrange that.
7. Yes, I believe that will work out (good, well).
8. Thank you, doctor. That will be (good, well) for my schedule, too.
9. Fong, (can, may) we have these stacks of old magazines?
10. Of course you (can, may), Shelly.
11. Are you sure you (can, may) carry them, though?
12. I (can, may) help you if they are too heavy for you.
13. Thank you, Juan, but I'm sure that I (can, may) manage very (good, well).
14. That's a (good, well) money-making project you have. What is the money being used for?
15. We're raising money for new school band uniforms, and we're doing quite (good, well), too.
16. Susan did a (good, well) job on her science project.
17. She did so (good, well) that she will take her project to the science fair this summer.
18. She will also bring a guest with her, and she has a (good, well) idea who she will bring.
19. If Alan (can, may), he will do a project and go with her.

Unit 3, Grammar and Usage

Lesson 43

Using *Teach/Learn* and *Set/Sit*

- Teach means "to give instruction to others."
    EXAMPLE: Rosa will **teach** me to speak Spanish.
- Learn means "to get knowledge."
    EXAMPLE: I'm **learning** to speak Spanish.
- Set means "to place something in a special position."
    EXAMPLE: Please **set** the books on the table.
- Sit means "to take a resting position."
    EXAMPLE: Please **sit** down and rest for a minute.

■ **Underline the correct word in each sentence below.**

1. Andy: Who will (learn, teach) you to play the piano?

2. Pat: I hope to (learn, teach) from my sister, Beth.

3. Andy: Wouldn't it be better to have Ms. Hill (learn, teach) you?

4. Pat: You were quite small when she began to (learn, teach) you.

5. Pat: Was it hard to (learn, teach) when you were so young?

6. Andy: Yes, but Ms. Hill let me (set, sit) on a high, round stool.

7. Andy: At home I would (set, sit) a thick book on the piano bench
    and (set, sit) on it.

8. Andy: Then I grew enough so that I could (set, sit) on the bench
    and still reach the keys.

9. Liz: Beth asked Marty to (learn, teach) her how to drive.

10. Liz: She says it would make her nervous to have someone that
    she didn't know (learn, teach) her.

11. Tom: Are you going to go along and (set, sit) in the back seat?

12. Liz: I doubt that Beth will want me to (set, sit) anywhere
    near when she is driving.

13. Scott: Martha, I am going to (learn, teach) you a new skill.

14. Scott: I know you are old enough to (learn, teach) how
    to (set, sit) the table.

15. Scott: (Set, Sit) there, Martha, so that you can watch me.

16. Scott: First I (set, sit) the plates in their places.

17. Scott: Then I put a glass at each place where someone will (set, sit).

18. Scott: Once I (learn, teach) you everything, you will be able
    to (set, sit) the table every night.

19. Martha: Good! Let me try to (set, sit) it now.

A. Write each noun, pronoun, verb, and adjective from the sentences below in the proper column.

1. Kathy found Ray's black science notebook.

2. She gave it to him on Thursday.

3. He was thankful.

NOUNS	PRONOUNS	VERBS	ADJECTIVES
_____	_____	_____	_____
_____	_____	_____	_____
_____	_____	_____	_____
_____	_____	_____	_____

B. Underline each verb or verb phrase in the present tense. Circle each verb or verb phrase in the past tense. Then write the future tense of each verb.

1. On that television series, we study people of other lands. _____

2. On the first program, we learned about the people of Egypt. _____

3. Old records tell us that the people ploughed with a crooked stick. _____

4. They grew crops in the sand. _____

5. Some farmers raised wheat and barley. _____

C. Circle the correct verb in parentheses.

1. The parakeet had (sang, sung) in its cage all day.
2. Marilyn had (saw, seen) it do this before.
3. Once when she had (gone, went) out, she returned to find it singing.
4. The bird (did, done) its best singing in the afternoon.
5. Marilyn looked out the window and (seen, saw) why.
6. Another bird (sang, sung) back to her parakeet.

 Unit 3, Grammar and Usage

D. Write the correct form of the verb in parentheses.

1. (eat)   Rowena had just _____ breakfast.

2. (break) Suddenly, the window in the living room _____ .

3. (fall)   Rosa almost _____ out of her chair in surprise.

4. (begin) She had _____ to get up when she heard another noise.

5. (throw) It sounded as though somebody had _____ something in the window.

6. (give)   She _____ the police a call.

7. (steal)   They asked if anything was _____ .

8. (write)   They _____ down the information she gave them.

9. (take)   Soon they had _____ down everything she knew.

10. (drink)   Rosa _____ a glass of water and waited for them to come.

E. Underline each prepositional phrase. Circle each adverb.

1. The police arrived shortly at Rosa's house.

2. They closely inspected the window and went around the house.

3. Rosa excitedly told them that she was too upset by it.

4. They quietly assured her that she was safe in her house.

5. The noise was made by a squirrel carelessly throwing shells.

6. Rosa waved happily at the officers as they left the scene of the crime.

F. Circle the correct word in each sentence below.

1. James (sit, set) his tape recorder on the table.

2. "I didn't know it would be so hard to (learn, teach) a new language," he said.

3. "I hope I (may, can) understand Spanish by the time we leave for Mexico."

4. "You have always been a (well, good) student," said Phillip.

5. "I hope you will (learn, teach) me some things, too."

6. "Believe me," said James, "if I (teach, learn) it (good, well) enough, I will (set, sit) you down and (teach, learn) you what I know."

A. Underline the correct word in each sentence below.

1. Someone who can't see (doesn't, don't) have to depend on another person.
2. Dog trainers (can, may) teach dogs to be their dependable guides.
3. These dogs leave (their, theirs) kennels at ten weeks of age.
4. Each puppy stays in a 4-H club (members, member's) home.
5. One member, Karen, had (her, hers) puppy, Koko, for twelve months.
6. Karen had always (wanted, will want) a puppy to take care of.
7. But, Karen had to realize that Koko was not really (her, hers).
8. "Koko and (I, me) hated to say goodbye," Karen said.
9. "It was hard to tell which one of us was (sadder, saddest)."
10. Karen had (learned, taught) Koko to walk on a leash and to display normal, (good, well) behaviour.
11. The kennel owner said Karen had done her job (good, well).
12. He knew that Koko could now (learn, teach) to guide someone who couldn't see.
13. Now Karen (goes, went) to the kennel every week to visit Koko.
14. She has (took, taken) a treat for him each time, and Koko always wags his tail to say thank you.
15. Koko is (largest, larger) each time Karen sees him.

B. Read the paragraph below. Find and underline the eight errors in grammar and usage. In the space above the sentences, write the correction.

Dinosaur Provincial Park is located in Albertas badlands.

It have many fossils of the dinosaurs that roamed

around the area more than 100 million years ago.

Dinosaurs are among the larger animals that

ever lived. Some dinosaurs was meat eaters.

Other's ate only plants. Albertosaurus was one

of the fiercer of them all. Him and

tyrannosaurus rex were both big and

dangerous. Scientists do not know what

colour their skin were.

C. In the paragraph below, underline each adjective. Circle each adverb.

Marlena sat up in her small bed. She yawned

broadly, and gazed out of the bedroom window. Multicoloured

lights danced crazily in the dark sky.

Marlena quickly rubbed her sleepy eyes and looked

again. The mysterious lights still shimmered.

"These must be the northern lights," she

whispered quietly to herself.

D. Complete this paragraph about the circus by writing adjectives or adverbs in the blanks.

The _____ snow falls _____ . The

_____ children make snowmen. They laugh _____

at the _____ faces they make. They _____

feel the _____ wind on their _____ cheeks as they

play. One _____ boy throws a snowball at his friend.

But the friend ducks _____ and the snowball

lands _____ on the ground.

E. Write the correct possessive form of each noun in parentheses.

1. (play)   The _____ subject is family life.

2. (actors)   All of the _____ parts are as family members.

3. (children) Two of the _____ roles are played by real brothers.

4. (parent)   One _____ job takes her out of town a great deal.

5. (audience) The _____ applause lasted for five minutes.

F. Underline the correct word in parentheses in each sentence below.

1. The mystery of the play is the (harder, hardest) to solve
   of any mystery I've read.

2. Why does the sun shine (brighter, brightest) in that village
   than at the other village?

3. This play has a (more, most) surprising ending than the other play.

> ■ **Capitalize** the first word of a sentence.
>   EXAMPLE: Many people have pen pals.
> ■ Capitalize the first word of a direct quotation.
>   EXAMPLE: Jane asked, "Where does your pen pal live?"

A. Circle each letter that should be capitalized. Write the capital letter above it.

1. "have you met your pen pal?" I asked.

2. john answered, "yes, he spent the holidays with me."

3. so I've invited my pen pal to visit me.

4. he hopes to arrive in my country next June.

5. i am making many plans for his visit.

6. we're going to hike in the mountains.

> ■ Capitalize the first word of every line of poetry.
>   EXAMPLE: There was a monkey climbed up a tree;
>   When he fell down, then down fell he.
> ■ Capitalize the first, last, and all important words in the titles
>   of books, poems, stories, and songs.
>   EXAMPLE: Who wrote *Little House on the Prairie*?

B. Circle each letter that should be capitalized. Write the capital letter above it.

1. there was an old woman

   lived under a hill,

   and if she's not gone,

   she lives there still.

2. if all the world were water,

   and all the water were ink,

   what should we do for bread and cheese?

   and what should we do for drink?

3. Have you read Dennis Lee's poem "garbage delight"?

4. We are learning the song "farewell to nova scotia."

5. If you're interested in ballooning, read *up, up and away*.

6. Mike wrote a story called "a balloon ride."

Lesson
45

Capitalizing Proper Nouns and Adjectives

- Capitalize all proper nouns.
  EXAMPLES: Main Street, Germany, Atlantic Ocean, Friday, New Brunswick, Rocky Mountains, Passover, December, Aunt Ann, Mom, Holmes School, James
- A proper adjective is an adjective that is made from a proper noun. Capitalize all proper adjectives.
  EXAMPLES: the English language, Italian dishes, French people, American tourists, the Australian cities

A. Circle each letter that should be capitalized. Write the capital letter above it.

1. My friend larry had just returned from a world trip.

2. He brought gifts for everyone in my family, including my

   dog, chipper.

3. He gave my mother some delicate japanese dishes that he

   bought in tokyo, japan.

4. He gave my sister a Scottish plaid kilt like the bagpipers

   wear in Scotland.

5. My father really likes the hat larry got for him in london.

6. The hat reminds us of the kind Sherlock holmes wore.

7. My gift was an african drum from mali in west africa.

8. larry told us how delicious the italian food was.

9. chipper's gift was a colourful, embroidered dog jacket

   from thailand.

B. Write four sentences about a trip you would like to take. Use proper nouns and at least one proper adjective in the sentences.

1. _____

2. _____

3. _____

4. _____

> ■ Capitalize a person's title when it comes before a name.
>   EXAMPLES: Mayor Thomas, Premier Swanson
> ■ Capitalize abbreviations of titles.
>   EXAMPLES: Dr. Namis; Mr. and Mrs. J. B. Benton, Jr.; Ms.
>   Harris; Mr. John F. Lynch, Sr.

A. Circle each letter that should be capitalized. Write the capital letter above it.

1. We saw sergeant potter and mayor lan in the

   office.

2. They were discussing something important with dr. laura

   bedford and councillor carol phillips.

3. We ate lunch with rev. barton and mr. james adams, jr.

4. They are part of a committee planning a welcome for prince

   Charles of England, who will tour our province next month.

> ■ Capitalize abbreviations of days and months, parts of
>   addresses, and titles of members of the armed forces. Also
>   capitalize all letters in postal codes and abbreviations for
>   provinces.
>   EXAMPLES: Mon.; Sept.; 501 Elm St. N.; Capt. W. R.
>   Russell; Perth, ON, J6B 4L2

B. Circle each letter that should be capitalized. Write the capital letter above it.

1. gen. david e. morgan

   6656 n. second ave.

   trenton, on k8v 5x2

2. valentine's day Exhibit

   at oak grove library

   mon.–fri., feb 10–14

   101 madison st. e.

3. sgt. carlos m. martinez

   17 watling st.

   shropshire SY7 OLW, england

4. maxwell school Field Day

   wed., apr. 30, 1:00

   Register mon.–tues., apr. 28–29

   mr. modica's office

- Use a **period** at the end of a declarative sentence.
  EXAMPLE: The lens is an important part of a camera.
- Use a **question mark** at the end of an interrogative sentence.
  EXAMPLE: Do you enjoy having your picture taken?

A. Add the correct end punctuation to each sentence below.

1. Photography is an exciting hobby for many people

2. My friend Karen is one of those people

3. Have you ever gone on a vacation with a camera bug

4. Craig and I love Karen's photos

5. But getting those really good shots can be tiring

6. Can you imagine waiting in the hot desert sun while Karen
   gets just the right angle on a cactus

7. Or have you ever sat in the car while your friend waited
   for a grazing elk to turn its head

8. I don't need so much time when I take pictures

9. Of course my pictures aren't always as good as Karen's

B. Add the correct end punctuation where needed in the paragraphs below.

Have you ever wondered what it would be like to live as
the early European settlers did___ You can visit log homes made to
look like the original cabins of these settlers___ Then you can
see how difficult life was for the pioneers who helped Canada to
grow___

The cabins were small and roughly built___ Many cabins had
just one room___ Where was the kitchen___ Most of the cooking was
done in the large fireplace___ The fireplace also supplied the
only heat___ Wasn't it cold___ You can be sure the winter winds
whistled between the logs___ And where did the settlers sleep___
Most cabins had a ladder reaching up to the bedroom loft___

The furniture in the cabins was usually as roughly built as
the cabins themselves___ All the clothing was handmade by the
family___ They ate food grown and caught on their land___ Would
you have liked to live in those times___

> - Use a period at the end of an imperative sentence.
>   EXAMPLE: Please sign your name here.
> - Use an **exclamation point** at the end of an exclamatory sentence.
>   EXAMPLE: What a wonderful time we had at the show!

C. Add the correct end punctuation to each sentence below.

1. A group of friends decided to go ice skating___

2. Terry asked, "Is Thursday okay with all of you___"

3. Carmen said, "It sounds great to me___"

4. They all agreed to meet at the lake___

5. Elaine said, "Wow, is it ever cold___"

6. "Get moving," said Leon. "You'll warm right up___"

7. They skated for several hours___

8. Terry asked, "Who's ready to sit close to a warm fire___"

9. Carmen said, "I thought you'd never ask___"

10. Suddenly she was hit by a snowball___

11. "Hey___" she shouted. "What's the big idea___"

12. Elaine laughed and said, "It's not that cold out___"

D. Add the correct end punctuation where needed in the paragraphs below.

Oh, how I hate mosquitoes___ Pass me the fly swatter___ They seem to be everywhere at this time of year___ it is hard to find anything good to say about them___

Only the female mosquito bites human beings___ Don't worry about the males___ Explain to me how to tell the difference___ And why do all the females seem to end up near me___

Do you want to know more___ In some countries, mosquitoes carry serious diseases, like malaria___ What a scary thought___ Where can we go to get away from them___ Mosquitoes live in all kinds of climates, I'm afraid___ There are even some that can survive the harsh winters in the Arctic___

> - Use **quotation marks** to show the exact words of a speaker. Use a comma or other punctuation marks to separate the quotation from the rest of the sentence.
>   EXAMPLE: "Who made this delicious candy?" asked Claire.
> - A quotation may be placed at the beginning or the end of a sentence. It may also be divided within the sentence.
>   EXAMPLES: Lawrence said, "Let's play checkers." "My brother," said Leslie, "brought me this ring."

A. Add quotation marks to each sentence below.

1. We will read about a great inventor today, said Miss Davis.

2. Let me see, Miss Davis went on, whether you can guess who the inventor is.

3. Will you give us some clues? asked Chris.

4. Yes, answered Miss Davis, and here is the first clue.

5. His inventions have made our lives easier and more pleasant, said Miss Davis.

6. Is it Alexander Graham Bell? asked Judy.

7. Mr. Bell did give us the telephone, said Miss Davis, but he is not the man I have in mind.

8. This man gave us another kind of machine that talks, Miss Davis said.

9. It must be Thomas Alva Edison and the phonograph, said Jerry.

10. You are right, Miss Davis said.

B. Place quotation marks and other punctuation where needed in the sentences below.

1. Polly asked Where will you spend the holidays, Michelle?

2. We plan to drive to Henry's ranch said Michelle.

3. Polly asked Won't it be quite cold?

4. Yes said Michelle but it will be so much fun to slide down the hill behind the house.

5. It's great fun to go into the woods and cut down a Christmas tree added Bob.

6. Come with us said Michelle.

> ■ Use an **apostrophe** in a contraction to show where a letter
>   or letters have been taken out.
>   EXAMPLE: I **can't** be there until three o'clock.
> ■ Use an apostrophe to form a possessive noun. Add -'s to
>   most singular nouns. Add -' to most plural nouns.
>   EXAMPLE: Mike's gym shoes are high tops. The men's suits are
>   blue and white.

■ **Write the word or words in which an apostrophe has been left out.**
  Insert the apostrophe.

1. Building a new homes the dream of many people.   _____ home's _____

2. It can also become a persons worst nightmare. _____

3. Cant you see that planning carefully is the key? _____

4. If you dont plan everything, somethings bound to _____

   go wrong. _____

5. Youd better start by finding out how many rooms _____

   youll need. _____

6. An architects advice may also be helpful. _____

7. Getting many opinions can help you decide whats best. _____

8. But youd better already have some idea before you _____

   begin, or you'll have problems. _____

9. Find out everyones wishes for their rooms. _____

10. Others ideas may be completely different from your own. _____

11. If you talk it over, everyones ideas can be used. _____

12. You wouldnt want to end up with a home youre _____

    completely unhappy with. _____

13. After all, your homes the place where youll be spending _____

    most of your time. _____

Using Commas in Sentences

- Use a **comma** between words or word groups in a series.
  EXAMPLE: Food, medical supplies, blankets, and clothing were rushed to the flooded area.
- Use a comma to separate the parts of a compound sentence.
  EXAMPLE: Many homes were flooded, and the owners were taken to safety in boats.

A. Add commas where needed in the sentences below.

1. The heavy rain caused flooding in Chicoutimi Jonquiére Boilleau and other towns along the Saguenay River.

2. The flood washed away bridges roads and some small homes.

3. Our home had water in the basement and most of our neighbours' homes did, too.

4. We spent the night bailing mopping and worrying.

5. We put our washer and dryer up on blocks and then we helped Elise.

6. Some of our shrubs flowers and small trees may have to be replaced.

7. Elise's newly-planted vegetable garden was washed away and the Bergerons lost their shed.

8. The people in our neighbourhood were very lucky and everyone agreed that the flood brought us closer together.

- Use a comma to separate a direct quotation from the rest of a sentence.
  EXAMPLE: "We're leaving now," said Ann. Ann said, "It's time to go."

B. Add commas where needed in the sentences below.

1. Sally asked "Why did the rooster cross the road?"

2. "To get to the other side " answered Terry.

3. "That's really an old joke " Terry added.

4. Sally asked "Do you know a newer one?"

5. Terry asked "What holds the moon up?"

6. "Moon beams" said Terry.

> - Use a comma to set off the name of a person who is addressed .
>   EXAMPLE: "Alan, can't you go with us?" asked Bill.
> - Use a comma to set off words like <u>yes</u>, <u>no</u>, <u>well</u>, and <u>oh</u> when they begin a sentence.
>   EXAMPLE: "No, I have to visit my aunt," answered Alan.

C. Add commas where needed in the sentences below.

1. "Melody and Tim would you like to go to the hockey game?" Marie asked.
2. "Oh yes!" Tim exclaimed.
3. "Marie I'd love to," called Melody.
4. "Well it's settled," said Marie.
5. "Ted did you go to the model show last night?" asked Sam.
6. "No I couldn't make it," answered Ted.
7. "Oh I was going to ask if Costa won a prize," Sam said.
8. "Well I hope so," Ted said.
9. "Well then," Sam said, "let's call and ask him."
10. "Costa did you win a prize last night?" Sam asked.
11. "Yes I did," replied Costa.
12. "Oh what did you win?" asked Sam.
13. "Well you'd never guess," answered Costa.
14. "Costa don't keep us guessing," said Sam.
15. "Well you know my model was of a helicopter. My prize was a ride in a helicopter!" exclaimed Costa.

D. Pretend that you and your friends are planning an outing. Write a conversation that might take place between you and your friends. Use the names of the persons being addressed. In some sentences, use <u>yes</u>, <u>no</u>, <u>oh</u>, or <u>well</u>. Punctuate your sentences correctly.

_____

_____

_____

_____

_____

_____

A. Circle each letter that should be capitalized. Write the capital letter above it.

1. last summer we toured alberta and montana.

2. my friend bob liked hiking in the rocky mountains.

3. the trip down the columbia river was my favourite part.

4. we spotted two american bald eagles.

5. i liked glacier park best.

6. bob bought a book named *a hiker's guide*.

7. dr. vicenik is premier adams's personal doctor.

8. mr. vicenik and mrs. morrison are brother and sister.

9. ms. louis has invited dr. vicenik's son to speak to our group.

10. we made a poster with this information on it:

    walter vicenik will speak

    at Winston school

    on tues., apr. 25 at 3:00

B. Add the correct end punctuation to each sentence below.

1. I love to walk on the beach___

2. Look at that sunset___

3. Have you ever seen anything so beautiful___

4. The waves sound so soft lapping in on the sand___

5. Take a picture of me___

6. Shall I take one of you___

7. Look, there's a starfish___

8. I've never seen one before___

9. Don't pick it up___

10. It belongs in the sea___

C. Add commas, quotation marks, and apostrophes where needed in each sentence below.

1. Mark do you know where George is? asked Donna.

2. No I dont answered Mark.

3. Hes supposed to meet you Kiko and me here she said.

4. Mark asked Why didnt you tell us?

5. I did! Donna exclaimed. Dont you remember our talk yesterday?

6. Oh now I do said Mark.

7. Donna said Ill bet George didnt remember.

8. Heres Kiko. At least she remembered and shes ready to help plan the fundraiser said Donna.

9. Oh Im sure George will be here said Mark.

10. Hes always ready to meet new people talk and help others out.

D. Correct the letter below. Circle each letter that should be capitalized. Add missing commas, periods, quotation marks, and apostrophes. Be sure to write the correct end punctuation on the blank after each sentence.

955 rimfire rd s

humboldt sk s0k 2b1

aug 25 1997

dear jose

    i cant wait to see you___ its going to be great visiting mexico city i know its now one of the largest cities in the world___ i cant imagine such a huge place___

    when i went to see dr fulton for my shots, he said eric my boy dont worry about anything___ mexico is a wonderful place to visit___ ive been there many times and always enjoyed myself___

    i said dr fulton did you ever get lost trying to find your way around ___ he said he hadnt but he also always had a good guide___ im glad ill have you there to show me around___

    honestly jose youve got to know how exciting this is___ i want to see everything do everything and learn everything i can about your country___

your friend

eric

A. Correct the story below. Circle each letter that should be capitalized. Add missing periods, question marks, exclamation points, commas, quotation marks, or apostrophes where needed. Be sure to write the correct end punctuation on the blank after each sentence.

have you ever read eugene fields poem, "the duel"___
The chinese plate and the old dutch clock told the story
to a poet ___ they were hanging above the fireplace and
they could see the gingham dog and the calico cat sitting
on the table ___

the gingham dog said bow-wow-wow ___

mee-ow answered the calico cat ___

then the dog and the cat began to fight ___ bits of gingham
and calico were scattered everywhere ___

the chinese plate cried oh what can we do ___
but the dog and cat continued to tumble and fight all night ___
the next morning there was no trace of dog or cat ___

many people said burglars must have stolen them ___
but the old chinese plate said to the poet they ate each
other up and thats the truth ___

what a surprise ending that was ___

B. Make corrections in the story below as you did in Exercise A.

There is a russian folktale named "the coming of the snow
maid ___ " it tells about winter in russia where winter is very
long and very cold ___

ivan, a peasant, and his wife, marie, had no children ___ they
often watched their neighbours children at play in the snow ___
one day marie got an idea ___

ivan lets make a snow child she said ___ we can pretend
it is our own ___

the snow child came alive and they called her Snow Maid ___
she grew rapidly until early june ___ then she disappeared
in a tiny cloud___

dont cry marie said ivan ___ Snow Maid has returned to the
sky but she will come back to us next september ___

C. Correct the story below. Circle each letter that should be capitalized. Write the capital letter above it. Add missing periods, commas, quotation marks, or apostrophes where needed. Be sure to write the correct end punctuation on the blank after each sentence.

Who would have thought that a 21-year-old boy who had

lost a leg to cancer would become a national hero___

he and his siblings, fred darrell and judith grew up near

vancouver, british columbia___

While at mcgill university, terry started having pains in one knee___

his doctors diagnosis was bone cancer and his leg had to be

amputated___ while he recovered, he got the

idea of running across canada in what he called a

Marathon of Hope to raise money for cancer research___

Foxs run started in st. johns, newfoundland. at first he

didnt get much attention but as time went on, the

young mans will drive and heart captured the countrys imagination___ in

toronto he got a heros welcome and people cheered him in every small

town he passed___

terrys run ended in thunder bay, ont, but he lives on

in the hearts of canadians___ a mountain was named

in his honour and every year people take part in the terry

fox run to continue terrys dream___

D. Write a paragraph about a Canadian hero or someone you know and admire. Follow all the rules of capitalization and punctuation.

_____

_____

_____

_____

_____

    Unit 4, Capitalization and Punctuation

Writing Sentences

> - Every sentence has a base. The **sentence base** is made up of a simple subject and a simple predicate.
>   EXAMPLE: <u>Men</u> <u><u>stared</u></u>.
> - Add other words to the sentence base to expand the meaning of the sentence.
>   EXAMPLE: The **bewildered** men stared **in amazement at the mysterious light**.

A. Expand the meaning of each sentence base below. Add adjectives, adverbs, and/or prepositional phrases. Write your expanded sentence.

1. (Plane flew.) _____

2. (Creatures ran.) _____

3. (Dogs played.) _____

4. (Police chased.) _____

5. (Girls discovered.) _____

B. Imagine two different scenes for each sentence base below Write an expanded sentence to describe each scene you imagine.

1. (Children explored.) a. _____

   b. _____

2. (Fire was set.) a. _____

   b. _____

3. (Crowd roared.) a. _____

   b. _____

4. (Wind blew.) a. _____

   b. _____

5. (Friend sent.) a. _____

   b. _____

6. (Actor was dressed.) a. _____

   b. _____

> - A **topic sentence** is a sentence that states the main idea of a paragraph.
>   EXAMPLE: **Many of the best things in life are free**. The sun and the moon give their light without charge. A true friend can't be bought. The beauty of the clouds in a blue sky is there for all to enjoy.

A. Write a topic sentence for each of the paragraphs below.

1. The summer had been extremely hot and dry. Many brush fires had broken out. People were told not to water their lawns or wash their cars. People responded by using less water and being careful about how they used water. Everyone realized the new rules were in the best interest of everyone.

TOPIC SENTENCE: _____

2. Nancy read everything she could find about nursing. She spent hours in the library learning about first aid. When the call came for summer volunteers at the hospital, she was the first to sign up. She was determined to prepare herself as best she could for what she hoped would be her career.

TOPIC SENTENCE: _____

3. There are many parks to enjoy. Museums and aquariums have interesting exhibits. Large stores and malls have a great selection of things to buy. Many large cities also have major sports teams to watch.

TOPIC SENTENCE: _____

B. Choose one of the topics below. Write a topic sentence for it. Then write a paragraph of about fifty words in which you develop the topic.

The most useful invention   My favourite holiday

A frightening experience   A place I want to visit

_____

_____

_____

_____

_____

_____

_____

Writing Supporting Details

> ■ Sentences that contain **supporting details** develop the topic sentence of a paragraph. The details may be facts, examples, or reasons.

A. Read the topic sentence below. Then read the numbered sentences. Underline the four sentences that contain details that support the topic sentence.

TOPIC SENTENCE: Automobile seat belts save lives.

1. The first seat belts didn't have shoulder straps.
2. A seat belt helps keep a front-seat passenger from going through the windshield.
3. A passenger who doesn't fasten his or her seat belt may be hurt if the car is in an accident.
4. Seat belts protect small children from falls and bumps while riding in the back seat.
5. Some cars today have automatic seat belts.
6. Studies on the number of lives saved prove the value of wearing seat belts.

B. Underline the correct word to complete the sentence.

The supporting details in the sentences above were (facts, examples, reasons).

C. Choose one of the topic sentences. Write it on the first line. Then write three sentences that contain supporting details. The details may be facts, examples, or reasons.

1. Having a pet is a lot of work.
2. A large (or small) family has advantages.
3. My vacation (in the mountains, at camp, on the seashore, or other place) was fun.
4. Every student should have an allowance.

_____

_____

_____

_____

D. Fill in the blank below with the word <u>facts</u>, <u>examples</u>, or <u>reasons</u>.

The supporting details in my paragraph were _____ .

- **Comparing** two objects, persons, or ideas shows the likenesses between them. Comparing expresses a thought in a colourful, interesting way.

  EXAMPLE: Walking lets the walker be as free as a bird that has flown from its cage.

- **Contrasting** two objects, persons, or ideas shows the differences between them. Contrasting can also express a thought in a colourful, interesting way.

  EXAMPLE: Baby Rachel's morning mood is one of sunshine, rainbows, and laughter. Her nap-time mood, however, suggests gathering clouds.

A. Read each topic sentence and the pair of sentences that follow. Underline the sentence that expresses a supporting detail in a colourful, interesting way.

1. TOPIC SENTENCE: Having the flu is no fun.

   a. Pat was tired of being in bed with the flu.

   b. After a week in bed with the flu, Pat felt like her pet hamster, Hamby, spinning his wheel in his cage.

2. TOPIC SENTENCE: Koalas aren't all they seem to be.

   a. A koala is cute but unfriendly.

   b. A koala looks like a cuddly teddy bear, but it is about as friendly as a grizzly bear.

B. Rewrite each sentence below in a more colourful, interesting way. Use comparison or contrast.

1. A mosquito bite is itchy.

   _____

2. Taking a bus to a museum is fun.

   _____

3. Dogs are friendlier than cats.

   _____

4. Reading is a good way to spend your free time.

   _____

5. Stealing a base makes baseball exciting.

   _____

- Supporting details can be arranged in order of location.
  EXAMPLE: The sofa was **on the long wall to your right**.
  A table sat **at either end** of the sofa.

A. In the paragraph below, underline the words that show location.

I stood watching. <u>Below me</u> was the ball field. Across the
street from the ball field, men were building an apartment
house. Cement trucks were lined up along the street. They
were delivering concrete for the basement walls of the
apartment house. A kindergarten class was playing baseball
on the ball field. The wise teacher told the class to move
away from the street.

**B. Choose one of the scenes or objects below. Write a topic sentence
about it. Then write a paragraph of at least five sentences describing
the scene or object. Use words such as <u>above</u>, <u>ahead</u>, <u>around</u>, <u>behind</u>,
<u>next to</u>, <u>on top of</u>, and <u>under</u> to show location.**

Scenes: your street, your home, a garden
Objects: your bicycle, a car, your favourite book

_____

_____

_____

_____

_____

_____

_____

_____

_____

C. Underline the words you used to show location.

_____

Lesson 56 — Topic and Audience

> - The **topic** of a paragraph should be something the writer is interested in or familiar with.
>   EXAMPLES: school, animals, science, sports, hobbies
> - The **title** should be based on the topic.
> - The **audience** is the person or people who will read what is written.
>   EXAMPLES: classmates, readers of the class newspaper, family members

A. Suppose that the topic chosen is <u>sports</u>. Underline the sports topic below that you would most like to write about.

1. Is winning the most important thing in sports?

2. There are many reasons why tennis (or baseball, or swimming, or _____) is my favourite sport.

3. Sports can be an enjoyable family activity.

B. Think about the topic you underlined in Exercise A. Underline the audience below that you would like to write for.

1. your family

2. a coach

3. your best friend

C. Write a paragraph of about seventy words, using the sentence you underlined in Exercise A as your topic sentence. Write a title for your paragraph. Direct your paragraph to the audience you underlined in Exercise B.

_____

_____

_____

_____

_____

_____

- **Clustering** uses a special drawing that shows how ideas relate to one main topic. That topic is written in a centre shape. Other shapes contain the ideas. Lines show how the ideas are connected to the main topic.

EXAMPLE:

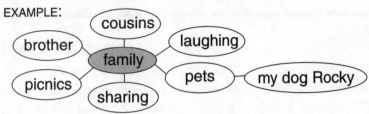

Topic Sentence—My family is wonderful.

A. Complete each cluster below by writing words that the topic makes you think of. You may add additional shapes and connecting lines.

1.

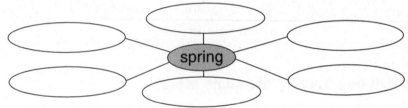

TOPIC SENTENCE: _____

2.

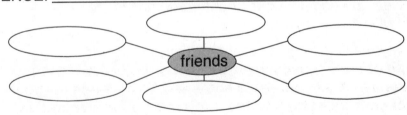

TOPIC SENTENCE: _____

B. Choose one of the topics in Exercise A. Write it on the title line below. Then write your topic sentence for that topic. Complete the paragraph.

_____

_____

_____

_____

_____

_____

A Descriptive Paragraph

> ■ A **descriptive paragraph** describes something. It is made
> colourful and interesting through the use of details.
>   EXAMPLE: A **thick coating** of dust covered everything in
>   the **old abandoned** house.

A. Read the descriptive paragraph below. Then answer the question.

> In my neighbourhood, there is a small grocery store just a
> block from my house. A retired couple, Mr. and Mrs. Aggens,
> are the owners. I always hope that Mrs. Aggens will wait on me.
> She is friendly and full of smiles. She always gives me extra
> large scoops of ice cream. She doesn't hurry me when I can't
> decide whether to spend my money on apples or fruit bars.
> After I make my purchase, I like to stay, smell the freshly
> ground coffee, and talk to Mrs. Aggens.

1. What kind of person is Mrs. Aggens? Underline the words that describe her.

crabby, patient, impatient, kind, stingy, generous

B. Read the paragraph below about the same store.

> In my neighbourhood, there is a store near our house. The owners
> are a husband and wife. The wife is patient, generous, and
> friendly. Near the door is a fruit counter and an ice cream
> counter. I often shop there.

1. List at least five details that are missing from this paragraph. _____

_____

_____

2. What is the result of leaving out these details? _____

_____

**C. Write a descriptive paragraph about a place you visit often.
Use details to make your paragraph colourful and interesting.**

_____

_____

_____

_____

> - Writers use **descriptive words** that tell how something looks, feels, smells, tastes, or sounds.
>   EXAMPLE: The **shady** forest was dressed in the **soft greens** and **pale yellows** of early spring.
> - Writers use verbs that tell exactly what someone is doing or how someone moves.
>   EXAMPLE: Richard **tramped** across the newly mopped kitchen floor.

A. Read the paragraph below, and answer the questions that follow.

Jody stood silently at the rickety gate of Harry's weathered old ranch house. The crooked gate hung on only its top hinge. The house that had never known a paintbrush seemed to have whitened with age. A gentle breeze rippled the tall grass and filled Jody's nostrils with the sugary smell of sweet peas. Jody turned. Yes, there were those lovely white, pastel pink, and lavender blooms. But everything else had faded with age.

1. What words tell how the ranch house looked? _____

how the gate looked? _____

2. What word tells how the breeze felt? _____

how the grass looked? _____ how it moved? _____

how the sweet peas smelled? _____ how they looked? _____

B. Choose a familiar place to write about in a descriptive paragraph. Write a topic sentence to begin the paragraph. Think about how the place looks, the sounds you might hear there, the smells you might smell there, how it feels to be there, and the things you might taste there. Write descriptive sentences that tell about these things to complete your paragraph.

_____

_____

_____

_____

_____

- **Revising** gives you a chance to rethink and review what you have written and to improve your writing. Revise by adding words and information, by deleting unneeded words and information, and by moving words, sentences, and paragraphs around.
- **Proofreading** involves checking spelling, punctuation, grammar, and capitalization. Use proofreader's marks to show changes needed.

Proofreader's Marks

≡	⊙	(sp)
Capitalize.	Add a period.	Correct spelling.
/	∧	¶
Make a small letter.	Add something.	Indent for new paragraph.
∧	℘	↷
Add a comma.	Take something out.	Move something.

A. Rewrite the paragraphs below. Correct the errors by using the proofreader's marks.

¶during the history of Earth‸there have been several ice ages⊙ these were times when giant sheets of ice spred across many parts of earth. People think that almost one third of the Land was covered by these hug sheets of ice.

The last ice age frozed so so much ocean water that the level of the oceans dropped. then lots of land apeared that usually lay underwater⊙When the tempeture began to warm up‸the ice sheets melted. The Ocean levels rose again.

_____

_____

_____

_____

_____

_____

_____

A. Expand the meaning of each sentence base below. Add adjectives, adverbs, and/or prepositional phrases. Write the expanded sentences.

1. (Reporter wrote.) _____

2. (Pilot flew.) _____

3. (Dentist drilled.) _____

4. (Crowd cheered.) _____

B. Write a topic sentence for the paragraph below.

   A car engine needs a radiator to stay cool. A radiator is a tank with thousands of openings for air to pass through. As the engine runs, hot water travels through hoses to the radiator. As the car moves, air cools the hot water in the radiator. When the car is stopped or moving slowly, a fan forces more air into the radiator.

TOPIC SENTENCE: _____

C. Read the topic sentence below. Then underline the three sentences that contain details supporting the idea of the topic sentence.

TOPIC SENTENCE: Many unique animals live in rain forests.

1. It is very hot in a rain forest.

2. Squirrel monkeys live in the rain forests of Central and South America.

3. Parrots and toucans sit in the trees and eat fruits and nuts.

4. I would like to see a rain forest.

5. Flying squirrels glide from tree to tree.

D. Write three supporting details for the following topic sentence. In the blank before each sentence, tell whether each is a fact, example, or reason.

TOPIC SENTENCE: There is too much violence on television today.

_____ 1. _____

_____ 2. _____

_____ 3. _____

E. Read the descriptive paragraph below. Then answer the questions.

From the window of the seaplane, Lucy spotted the island. It looked like an emerald in the middle of a shining turquoise sea. She immediately forgot the thundering sound of the propellers and the bouncy ride that she feared would give her a pounding headache. A sudden spray of sea water on the window startled her. As the plane drifted gently toward land, Lucy could almost smell the sea air. Bright pink and red flowers lined the sidewalks.

What words describe:

1. what the island looked like from the plane? _____

2. the sea? _____

3. the propellers? _____

4. how the plane moved toward land? _____

5. what colour the flowers were? _____

6. how the plane ride was? _____

7. what Lucy thought her headache might become? _____

8. the sea water on the window? _____

F. Rewrite the paragraph below. Correct the errors by following the proofreader's marks.

¶soils come in in two basic types, they are clay or sandy. Heavy soil, or clay, has small partikles that don't allow much air in. Sandy Soil is made of bigger pieces, and this tipe of soil pervides lots of air for plant roots. You should carfully study the soil type of you have befor you plant anything.

_____

_____

_____

_____

_____

A. Complete the cluster below. Write a title for the topic. Then write a topic sentence and three sentences that contain supporting details.

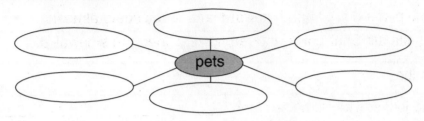

pets

_____

TOPIC SENTENCE: _____

_____

_____

_____

B. Write a paragraph of at least four sentences describing your living room, kitchen, or bedroom. Use location words such as <u>above</u>, <u>ahead</u>, <u>around</u>, <u>behind</u>, <u>next to</u>, <u>on top of</u>, and <u>under</u>.

_____

_____

_____

_____

C. Fill in the blanks in the paragraph below with descriptive words and action verbs that make the paragraph colourful and interesting.

The colt _____ pulled itself up on its _____

legs. Then it _____ after its mother. Just as the colt

neared the fence, a _____ , _____ rabbit

_____ under the fence and _____ up to the colt.

The startled colt _____ and let out a _____ neigh.

Its _____ mother _____ up to its side _____ .

D. Choose one of the topic sentences below. Write a paragraph of four sentences, using _reasons_ to support the thought of the topic sentence.

1. Everyone should learn to swim.
2. Laws are necessary.
3. Summer vacations are just the right length of time.

_____

_____

_____

E. Choose one of the topic sentences below. Write a paragraph of four sentences, using _examples_ to support the thought of the topic sentence.

1. Many television programs are educational.
2. Electrical inventions have made our lives easier.
3. A hobby is more than a way to take up time.

_____

_____

_____

_____

F. Read the paragraph below. Use proofreader's marks to revise and proofread the paragraphs. Then write your revised paragraph.

try to imagine what the world would be like if there were

no People in it. There would be no cities towns or

villages There would be no bildings of any knind. nobody

would be be there to do or make Anything.

_____

_____

_____

_____

_____

_____

Following Directions

■ When following written **directions**, it is important to read each step carefully. Be sure you have completed one step before going on to the next step.

■ **Read the recipe below. Then answer the questions that follow it.**

Peanut Butter Balls

125 mL wheat germ   125 mL powdered milk
125 mL sunflower seeds   125 mL honey
125 mL peanut butter   125 mL sesame seeds (if desired)

a. Spread wheat germ and sunflower seeds on a cookie sheet.
    Bake at 350° for 15 minutes, stirring every 5 minutes.

b. Place toasted wheat germ and sunflower seeds in a bowl.

c. Add all other ingredients except sesame seeds. Mix well.

d. Form into balls, using 1 teaspoonful of dough for each ball.

e. Roll balls in sesame seeds. (This step is not necessary.)

f. Chill for 3 hours.

g. Serve as a tasty, good-for-you snack or dessert.

1. What is the recipe for? _____

2. What kitchen utensils are needed? _____

3. What quantity of each ingredient is needed? _____

4. What ingredients are used in step <u>a</u>? _____

5. What should the oven temperature be? _____

6. How long should the wheat germ and sunflower seeds

    be baked? _____

7. How often should you stir the wheat germ and sunflower seeds

    while they are baking? _____

8. How much dough is needed to form each ball? _____

9. How long should the peanut butter balls be chilled before

    eating? _____

10. Which ingredient may be left out? _____

Unit 6, Study Skills   © 1997 Gage Educational Publishing Company   **83**

> ■ **Alphabetical order** is used in many kinds of listings.
>   EXAMPLE: Miss Clark's class list: Adams, Coss, Dukelow, Gutierrez, Lee, Rostov, Shapiro, Wong

A. Complete each sentence below.

1. The letter n comes after _____ and before _____ .

2. The letters between s and w are _____ .

> ■ Entries in a dictionary or an encyclopedia appear in alphabetical order, according to their first letters, second letters, third letters, and so on.
>   EXAMPLE: wave, wax, web, weed, wish, wisp

B. Number the words in each group in alphabetical order.

     3   4   2   1

1. whale, where, weary, water

2. school, second, safety, sailor

3. earth, ease, each, earn

4. recess, rain, ring, rose

C. Number the encyclopedia entries in each column in alphabetical order.

1. _____ Bell, Alexander Graham

2. _____ Berlin

3. _____ Bear

1. _____ Panda

2. _____ Pago Pago

3. _____ Panama Canal

> ■ Names in a telephone book are listed in alphabetical order, according to last names. When several people have the same last name, their names are arranged in alphabetical order, according to first names.
>   EXAMPLE: Barnes, John; Barnes, William; Barton, Clyde; Barwin, James D.

D. Copy the names in the order you would find them in a telephone book.

T. C. Caskey _____

Louis J. Caskey _____

Cindy Lyons _____

Paul Lyndale _____

      Unit 6, Study Skills

Dictionary: Guide Words

> ■ **Guide words** are words that appear at the top of each page
> in a dictionary. They show the first and last entry words on
> the page. Guide words tell whether an entry word is listed
> on that page.   EXAMPLE: **beets/beyond**: The word <u>begin</u>
> will appear on the page. The word <u>bid</u> will not.

**A. Read each pair of guide words and the list of entry words below.
Put a check in front of each entry word that would appear on the page.**

1. blade/bluff

_____ blur   _____ blast

_____ blink   _____ black

_____ blame   _____ blaze

_____ blossom   _____ blunder

_____ blush   _____ blouse

2. intend/island

_____ into   _____ invent

_____ instrument   _____ isn't

_____ introduce   _____ irrigate

_____ iron   _____ itch

_____ inward   _____ invite

**B. Read each pair of guide words and the list of entry words below. Circle
only the entry words that would appear on the page. Then write those
words in the order in which they would appear in the dictionary.**

1. meal/minister

meanwhile _____

melody _____

meadow _____

mention _____

mischief _____

2. product/provide

professor _____

propeller _____

proceed _____

program _____

protest _____

3. rear/rescue

recess _____

realize _____

recognize _____

reckon _____

receive _____

4. miserable/mitten

mist _____

mischief _____

miss _____

mite _____

mixture _____

Lesson
64 Dictionary: Syllables

- A **syllable** is each part of a word that is pronounced at one time.
- Dictionary entry words are divided into syllables to show how to divide a word at the end of a writing line.
- Put a **midline dot** (•) between syllables when dividing a word.
  EXAMPLE: a•wak•en

■ **Find each word in a dictionary. Write the word, placing a hyphen between syllables.**

1. chemical _____chem•i•cal_____
2. gasoline _____
3. degree _____
4. marvellous _____
5. disappear _____
6. chimney _____
7. continent _____
8. miserable _____
9. generally _____
10. glacier _____
11. arithmetic _____
12. exercise _____
13. hospital _____
14. problem _____
15. window _____
16. language _____
17. agriculture _____
18. parakeet _____
19. beginning _____
20. simple _____

21. determine _____
22. musician _____
23. salary _____
24. cheetah _____
25. interrupt _____
26. dentist _____
27. recognize _____
28. rascal _____
29. innocent _____
30. educate _____
31. achievement _____
32. darling _____
33. homestead _____
34. calendar _____
35. missionary _____
36. farewell _____
37. aluminum _____
38. bacteria _____
39. program _____
40. banana _____

Unit 6, Study Skills

Dictionary: Pronunciation

- Each dictionary entry word is followed by a respelling that shows how the word is **pronounced**, or said.
- **Accent marks** (′) show which syllables are said with the most stress.   EXAMPLE: au·to·mat·ic (ot′ ə mat′ ik)
- A **pronunciation key** (shown below) explains the other symbols used in the respelling.

A. Answer the questions below about the respelling of the word <u>automatic</u>. Use the pronunciation key at the right. (ot′ ə mat′ ik)

hat, āge, fär; let, ēqual, tėrm; it, īce; hot, ōpen, ôrder; oil, out; cup, pu̇t, rüle; əbove, takən, pencəl, lemən, circəs; ch, child; ng, long; sh, ship; th, thin; ŦH, then; zh, measure

1. What is the key word for the symbol <u>o</u>? _____

2. What is a key word for the symbol <u>ə</u>?   _____

3. What is the key word for the symbol <u>a</u>? _____

4. What is the key word for the symbol <u>i</u> ? _____

B. Use the pronunciation key as you look at each respelling. Underline the word for which the respelling stands.

1.	(ə ban′ dən)	ability	abandon	aboard
2.	(bak′ strōk′)	backstop	bakery	backstroke
3.	(klench)	clef	clench	clerk
4.	(dān′ tē)	daisy	dainty	dance
5.	(hīt)	height	hit	hint
6.	(en tīr′ lē)	entirely	entry	entertain
7.	(wiŦH′ ər)	whether	withhold	wither
8.	(noiz)	nosy	noise	nose
9.	(ot)	out	at	ought
10.	(wāt)	wit	white	weight
11.	(wȧl)	wall	walk	wail
12.	(vizh′ ən)	vision	visible	visit
13.	(frāt)	free	fright	freight
14.	(our)	hope	hour	ours
15.	(dī′ ə mənd)	demand	diamond	dime
16.	(sat′ ə līt′)	satisfy	salary	satellite
17.	(mī′ grāt)	mighty	migrate	migrant
18.	(ang′ gəl)	angry	angle	anger

> - A dictionary lists the **definitions** of each entry word. Many words have more than one definition. Sometimes a definition is followed by a sentence showing a use of the entry word.
> - A dictionary also tells the **part of speech** for each entry word. An abbreviation (shown below) stands for each part of speech.
>   EXAMPLE: **aunt** (ant or änt) *n.* **1** the sister of one's father or mother. **2** an uncle's wife.

A. Use the dictionary sample below to answer the questions.

au·di·ence (od´ e əns) *n.* **1** the people gathered to hear or see a performance or presentation: *The audience cheered the mayor's speech.* **2** the people reached by radio or television broadcasts, by books, etc.: *The book is intended for a juvenile audience.* **3** a chance to be heard; hearing: *The committee will give you an audience to hear your plan.* **4** a formal interview with a person of high rank: *The queen granted an audience to the famous singer.*

au·di·o·vis·u·al (od´ ē ō vizh´ ü əl) *adj.* of or having to do with both hearing and sight.

au·di·to·ri·um (od´ ə tô´ rē əm) *n.* **1** a large room for an audience in a theatre, school, etc.; large hall. **2** a building especially designed for lectures, concerts, etc.

au·di·to·ry (od´ ə tô´ rē) *adj.* of or having to do with hearing, the sense of hearing, or the organs of hearing: *the auditory nerve.*

1. How many definitions are given for the word

   audience? _____ for the words audiovisual and

   auditory _____ ? for the word auditorium? _____

2. Which part of speech does the abbreviation n.

   stand for? _____

3. Which part of speech is audiovisual and

   auditory? _____

4. Which words in the dictionary sample are

   nouns? _____

n.	noun
pron.	pronoun
v.	verb
adj.	adjective
adv.	adverb
prep.	preposition

B. Write the number of the dictionary definition used for the underlined word.

1. _____ At the end of the movie, the audience clapped loudly to show how much they had enjoyed it.

2. _____ All the Olympic gold medal winners were given an audience with the Prime Minister.

3. _____ The prisoner asked for an audience with the prison officials.

Lesson 67

Parts of a Book

- The **title page** tells the name of a book and the name of its author.
- The **copyright page** tells who published a book, where it was published, and when it was published.
- The **table of contents** lists the chapter or unit titles and the page numbers on which they begin. It is at the front of a book.
- The **index** gives a detailed list of the topics in a book. It gives the page numbers for each topic. It is at the back of a book.

A. Answer the questions below.

1. Where should you look for the page number of a particular topic? _____

2. Where should you look to find out who wrote a book? _____

3. Where should you look to find the name of a book? _____

4. Where should you look to find out who published a book? _____

5. Where should you look to get a general idea of the contents of a book? _____

6. Where should you look to find out when a book was published? _____

B. Use your *Language Power* book to answer the questions.

1. What is the title of this book? _____

2. On what page does Unit Five start? _____

3. List the pages that deal with revising and proofreading. _____

4. What is the copyright date of this book? _____

5. Who are the authors of this book? _____

6. On what page is the lesson on writing topic sentences? _____

7. Where is the index? _____

8. On what page does Unit Two start? _____

9. List the pages that deal with prepositions. _____

10. What lesson is on page 43? _____

Using an Encyclopedia

- An **encyclopedia** is a reference book that has articles on many different subjects. The articles are arranged in alphabetical order in different books, called volumes. Each volume is marked to show which subjects are inside.
- **Guide words** are used to show the first subject on each page.
- There is a listing of **cross-references** at the end of most articles to related subjects that the reader can use to get more information on that subject.

A. Read the sample encyclopedia entry below. Use it to answer the questions that follow.

> **WATER** is a liquid. Like air (oxygen), water is necessary for all living things. A person can live only a few days without water. Water is lost from the body every day and must be replaced. Drinking and eating replace water. About 60 percent of a person's body weight is water. *See also* OXYGEN.

1. What is the article about? _____

2. Why is water important? _____

3. How much of a person's body is water? _____

4. How is water in the body replaced? _____

5. What other subject could you look under to get more information? _____

6. What could be another related topic? _____

> **OXYGEN** is a gas that has no smell, no taste, and no colour. Nearly all living things need oxygen to live. Oxygen mixes with other things in a person's body to produce energy needed for life processes. Oxygen is also an important part of water. Oxygen is sometimes called air.

7. How are oxygen and water the same? _____

8. Does the above cross-reference mention water? _____

9. How does the article describe oxygen? _____

10. What is another word for oxygen? _____

- When looking for an article in the encyclopedia:
  Look up the last name of a person.
     EXAMPLE: To find an article on Ann Frank, look under <u>Frank</u>.
  Look up the first word in the name of a place.
     EXAMPLE: To find an article on New South Wales, look under <u>New</u>.
  Look up the most important word in the name of a general topic.
     EXAMPLE: To find an article on the arctic fox, look under <u>fox</u>.

B. Write the word you would look under to find an article on each of the following subjects.

1. Nellie McClung _____

2. salt water _____

3. North Pole _____

4. lakes in Scotland _____

5. Rio de Janeiro _____

6. United Kingdom _____

7. modern literature _____

8. breeds of horses _____

C. The example below shows how the volumes of one encyclopedia are marked. The volumes are numbered. The subjects are in alphabetical order. Write the number of the volume in which you would find each article.

A	B	C-CH	CI-CZ	D	E	F	G	H	I-J	K
1	2	3	4	5	6	7	8	9	10	11

L	M	N	O	P	Q-R	S	T	U-V	W-Z
12	13	14	15	16	17	18	19	20	21

_____ 1. caring for chickens

_____ 2. the flag of Canada

_____ 3. how glass is made

_____ 4. vitamins

_____ 5. reptiles

_____ 6. the history of Japan

_____ 7. how rainbows are formed

_____ 8. pine trees

A. Read the directions below. Then answer the questions that follow.

Take Highway 72 north to the Elm Street exit. Turn left, and cross the highway. Go to the first stop sign, beside the school. Turn right on Bluffside, and go to the second stoplight. Turn left. Go one block, and then turn right on Creekway. Peter's address is 1809 Creekway. His house is blue and sits at the top of the hill on the left.

1. Where do these directions take you? _____

2. How many left turns will you take? _____

3. What street is Peter's house on? _____

4. Which direction do you go on Highway 72? _____

5. What sign is by the school? _____

B. Use the sample dictionary page below to answer the questions that follow.

traffic / transatlantic

traf·fic (traf′ ik) *n.* **1** the people, automobiles, wagons, ships, etc. coming and going along a way of travel. **2** buying and selling; commerce; trade. **3** the business done by a railway line, a steamship line, etc. **4** the number of passengers or the amount of freight carried.

tram·ple (tram′ pəl) *v.* crush, destroy, violate, etc. by or as if by treading on heavily: *The cattle broke through the fence and trampled the farmer's crops.*

trance (trans) *n.* **1** a state of unconsciousness resembling sleep: *A person may be in a trance from*

illness, from the influence of some other person, or from his or her own will. **2** a dreamy, absorbed condition that is like a trance.

tran·quil (trang′ kwəl) *adj.* calm; peaceful; quiet: *a tranquil mood, the tranquil evening air.* —**tran′ quil·ly,** *adv.*

trans·at·lan·tic (tran′ sə tlan′ tik) *adj.* **1** crossing or extending across the Atlantic Ocean. **2** having to do with crossing the Atlantic Ocean: *transatlantic air fares.* **3** on the other side of the Atlantic Ocean.

1. What are the guide words? _____

2. Which word is a verb? _____ How is its pronunciation shown? _____

3. Which words are nouns? _____

_____

4. Which word has the most syllables? _____

5. Which word has only one syllable? _____

6. Which words are adjectives? _____

7. Which word means "to crush"? _____

8. What is the meaning of tranquil? _____

C. Use the sample encyclopedia entry to answer the questions.

LOCK Locks are sets of gates that help ships move through canals. Each lock is on a different level, and two sets of gates make up each lock. The locks are similar to stairs. A ship moves into a lock, and the gates in front of and behind the ship close. Water is then pumped into or let out of the enclosed lock. This raises or lowers the ship to the level of the next lock. See also CANAL.

1. What is the article about? _____

2. What do locks do? _____

3. How many sets of gates does a lock have? _____

4. What are locks compared to in the article? _____

5. What is the cross-reference? _____

D. The example below shows how the volumes of a small encyclopedia are marked. Circle the word you would look under to find an article on each of the following subjects. Then write the number of the volume in which you would find each article.

A-C	D-F	G-H	I-L	M-N	O-R	S-T	U-W	X-Z
1	2	3	4	5	6	7	8	9

_____ **1.** the history of mining

_____ **2.** Louis Riel

_____ **3.** the Nile River

_____ **4.** plant life of the tundra

_____ **5.** the capital of Sweden

_____ **6.** Great Danes

_____ **7.** Japanese gardens

_____ **8.** how volcanoes erupt

E. Write title page, copyright page, table of contents, or index to tell where to find this information.

_____ **1.** the author's name

_____ **2.** the page on which certain information can be found

_____ **3.** the year the book was published

_____ **4.** the page on which a certain chapter starts

_____ **5.** the company that published the book

A. Read the recipe below. Then answer the questions that follow.

Low-Calorie Buttermilk Dressing

45 mL lemon juice

6 mL seasoned salt

1 mL prepared mustard

250 mL buttermilk

Sugar

Combine all ingredients except sugar. Blend well. Add sugar to taste.
Pour on lettuce or spinach salad. Makes 250 mL.

1. How much sugar do you use? _____

2. How much does the recipe make? _____

B. Write the words below on the lines beside their respellings and definitions.

academy	accompany

_____ **1.** (ə kad′ ə mē) **1.** a private high school.
  2. a school giving training in a special field.

_____ **2.** (ə kump′ nē) **1.** to go along with.
  2. to perform a musical accompaniment for.

C. Read the guide words. Then write the words from the box that would be found on the same page, placing a midline dot between syllables.

slop/sneer

1. _____

2. _____

3. _____

sliding	smattering
slumber	sluggish
snuggle	
sliver	

D. Write title page, copyright page, table of contents, or index to tell where to find this information.

_____ **1.** the chapter titles in a book

_____ **2.** the year a book was published

_____ **3.** the page number on which a topic can be found

_____ **4.** the title of a book

E. Find the article for <u>butternut</u> in an encyclopedia. Then answer the following questions.

1. What encyclopedia did you use? _____

2. What are butternuts? _____

3. What is another name for butternut? _____

4. How are butternuts used? _____

5. How do butternuts grow? _____

6. In what countries are butternuts found? _____

7. What were the husks of butternuts used for? _____

8. Why were the husks good for spinning cloth? _____

9. Why do you think the cross-references are important? _____

10. Does the article mention the cross-references? _____

F. The example below shows how the volumes of one encyclopedia are marked. Circle the word under which you would look to find an article. On the first line, write the number of the volume you would look in to find the article. Then number the subjects in alphabetical order on the second lines.

A	B	C-CH	CI-CZ	D	E	F	G	H	I-J	K
1	2	3	4	5	6	7	8	9	10	11

L	M	N	O	P	Q-R	S	T	U-V	W-Z
12	13	14	15	16	17	18	19	20	21

_____ _____ 1. the city of Oslo

_____ _____ 2. kinds of vegetables

_____ _____ 3. Great Wall of China

_____ _____ 4. uses for boxcars

_____ _____ 5. uses of the snowshoe

_____ _____ 6. life cycle of the bee

_____ _____ 7. invention of the zipper

_____ _____ 8. life span of a monkey

_____ _____ 9. Walt Disney

_____ _____ 10. kinds of melons

_____ _____ 11. how aspirin is made

_____ _____ 12. lakes in Paraguay

Synonyms, Antonyms, and Homonyms ▪ Write <u>S</u> before each pair of synonyms. Write <u>A</u> before each pair of antonyms. Write <u>H</u> before each pair of homonyms.

1. _____ kind, cruel   5. _____ come, arrive   9. _____ I'll, aisle

2. _____ stop, halt   6. _____ build, destroy   10. _____ help, hurt

3. _____ been, bean   7. _____ beet, beat   11. _____ grow, increase

4. _____ together, apart   8. _____ take, seize   12. _____ here, there

Homographs ▪ Write the homograph for each pair of meanings below. The first letter of each word is given for you.

1. a. to be silent   b. a flower   m _____

2. a. to hit   b. a sweet drink   p _____

3. a. to be able   b. a tin container   c _____

4. a. part of the eye   b. student   p _____

5. a. to mix   b. to move around   s _____

6. a. a sharp point   b. to knock over   t _____

Prefixes and Suffixes ▪ Add a prefix or suffix from the box to the base words in parentheses. Write the new word in the blank.

re-   -ful   mis-   -less   un-   pre-   -able

1. Susan was (happy) _____ when her new computer didn't work.

2. She (read) _____ the directions.

3. She found that she had (understood) _____ them the first time.

4. It seemed the problem was (repair) _____ .

5. She was ready for a (view) _____ of what her computer could do.

6. Susan knew she would spend (end) _____ hours using it.

7. She knew her computer would be (depend) _____ .

8. She noticed that there were many (help) _____ programs on it.

Contractions ■ Write the two words that make up the contraction in each sentence.

_____ _____   1. "Let's go to the movies," said Janet.

_____ _____   2. "We've been two nights this week," said Tim.

_____ _____   3. "I'm just trying to catch up," said Janet.

_____ _____   4. "They've made so many I want to see."

_____ _____   5. Tim said, "We can't see all of them."

_____ _____   6. "Couldn't we try?" asked Janet, laughing.

Compound Words ■ Use the words below to form a compound word that will complete each sentence. Write the word on the line.

plant	water	stand	power	play	fall	mate	under

1. The beautiful _____ splashed into a clear pool below.

2. My little sister's favourite _____ is moving.

3. I couldn't _____ what he was saying.

4. The _____ produced large amounts of electricity.

Contractions and Compound Words ■ Underline the contractions, and circle the compound words in the paragraph. Then write each underlined or circled word and the two words from which it is made.

> I wondered what the firefighter was doing. He was standing in the roadway, but he wasn't directing traffic. I looked up, and in the treetop was a kitten. It couldn't get down. There was a woman standing by the tree. She was the owner of the kitten.

1. _____   _____

2. _____   _____

3. _____   _____

4. _____   _____

5. _____   _____

Recognizing Sentences ▪ Write <u>S</u> before each sentence.

1. _____ Many interesting facts about bees.

2. _____ Bees have five eyes.

3. _____ On about thirty grams of honey for fuel.

4. _____ Bees tell other bees the distance to pollen areas.

Types of Sentences ▪ Identify the types of sentences below by writing <u>D</u> before a declarative sentence, <u>IN</u> before an interrogative sentence, <u>IM</u> before an imperative sentence, and <u>E</u> before an exclamatory sentence.

1. _____ Did you know that there are 20 000 kinds of bees?

2. _____ There is so much to learn about bees!

3. _____ Tell me how many kinds of bees are found here in Canada.

4. _____ This book says there are about a thousand species

of bees living here.

5. _____ Do they all produce honey?

6. _____ can't believe only one species produces honey!

Subjects and Predicates ▪ Draw a line between the subject and the predicate in each sentence below. Underline the simple subject once. Underline the simple predicate twice.

1. Most Canadian bees live in tunnels underground.
2. An average bee can fly 25 km/h.
3. A worker honeybee makes about 50 g of honey in its lifetime.
4. Its lifetime is just one growing season.
5. Two hundred bees make about five hundred grams of honey in one season.
6. A waxy material is released by bees.
7. This material is used in candles and polishes.
8. Bees cannot defend themselves against other insects.
9. At least one kind of fly can kill them.
10. Robber flies kill bees with their piercing beaks.

Sentences

Compound Subjects and Predicates ▪ Draw a line between the complete subject and the complete predicate in each sentence. Underline each compound subject once and each compound predicate twice.

1. Planets and moons revolve around other bodies in space.

2. Mercury and Venus revolve around the sun in less than a year.

3. The nine planets in our solar system rotate and spin like tops.

Compound Sentences ▪ Write C before each compound sentence.

_____ 1. The dark clouds rolled in, and then it began to rain.

_____ 2. We were worried about the dogs.

_____ 3. They were outside, so we went to look for them.

_____ 4. We searched everywhere, but we couldn't find them.

_____ 5. They usually stayed home when the weather was bad.

_____ 6. Soon we heard scratching at the door.

_____ 7. We opened it, and they shook their wet coats all over us.

Run-On Sentences ▪ Separate the run-on sentences below. Rewrite them correctly on the lines.

1. Laura tried to fix her car she changed the oil, she put in a new air filter.

_____

2. It worked it ran well she had done a good job.

_____

Compound Sentences and Run-on Sentences ▪ Rewrite the paragraph. Combine simple sentences into compound sentences, and separate run-on sentences.

Sometimes we hop in the car when we get restless. We just drive wherever we choose. It's fun and relaxing, we laugh and forget about our problems. After a while we have gone far enough, we turn around and drive back home.

_____

_____

_____

_____

Singular, Plural, and Possessive Nouns ▪ Complete the chart below.
Write the forms called for in each column.

Singular Noun	Plural Noun	Singular Possessive	Plural Possessive
1. actor			
2. baby			
3. beach			
4. horse			
5. woman			
6. child			

Action Verbs and Linking Verbs ▪ Underline each verb or verb phrase in the sentences below.

1. The little Lion-Dog was once a palace guard dog in Tibet.
2. The Lion-Dog got its name because of the breed's thick,
    lionlike mane
3. Today, Lhasa apso is the name of the breed.
4. Mainly a companion or a show dog, the Lhasa apso will guard
    its master's home.
5. Lhasa apsos gaze out a window at each person that goes by.

Using Verbs Correctly ▪ Circle the correct verb in parentheses.

1. Jake and I (is, are) friends.
2. One year we (go, went) camping with our friends.
3. We thought it (sounds, sounded) like fun.
4. We all (throw, threw) out ideas about where to go.
5. That was where the problems (begin, began).
6. We (drawn, drew) straws to decide.
7. Tom (choose, chose) the longest one, so he got to pick.
8. We decided we would (taken, take) a trip to B.C.
9. We all decided that B.C. (was, were) an interesting
    place to visit.

Pronouns ▪ Underline each pronoun. Write <u>S</u> if it is a subject pronoun, <u>O</u> if it is an object pronoun, and <u>P</u> if it is a possessive pronoun.

_____ 1. Jake, are your suitcases packed yet?

_____ 2. I packed lots of summer clothes.

_____ 3. They will be great to wear on the trip.

_____ 4. Jake answered me by saying no.

_____ 5. Then Tom said he would help Jake pack.

_____ 6. Jake, Tom, Susan, and I finished right on time.

Adjectives and Adverbs ▪ Underline each adjective, and circle each adverb in the paragraph below.

After several hours, Jake began to talk quietly. He wondered what the most beautiful place in B.C. was. Susan said that Whistler was prettier than any other place. Tom loudly disagreed. He spoke knowingly of the rugged beauty and untouched splendour of the islands. Susan gently suggested that it had been a long time since he had been there. His wonderful memories might not be very accurate.

Prepositions ▪ Underline each prepositional phrase in the sentences below. Circle each preposition.

1. We got to a campsite at midnight.

2. The air smelled of pine trees.

3. In the morning, we explored the area near the site.

4. We saw a deer run through the forest.

5. We rested by a small creek for a while.

Using Words Correctly ▪ Circle the correct word in each sentence below.

1. If we (can, may), we will go all the way to the Peace River.

2. We are (learning, teaching) a great deal about B.C.

3. It's not easy to (set, sit) in a car for so long.

4. But it is still a (well, good) experience.

5. Seeing the province is (learning, teaching) us a lot.

6. We have learned our lessons very (good, well).

Capitalization ▪ Correct the sentences below. Circle each letter that should be capitalized. Write the capital letter above it.

1. i have always wanted to visit niagara falls.

2. jeri and i decided to go see them in march, before the crowds arrived.

3. we almost stayed in new brunswick because the bay of fundy was so beautiful.

4. fredericton was a wonderful town, named after prince frederick, the second son of king george III.

5. however, the book we were reading, *niagara daredevils* by mr. a. o'brien, convinced us to go on to ontario.

6. we stopped in montréal, québec, to send postcards back to our friends in newfoundland.

7. all jeri could talk about was riding on the *maid of the mist*, the boat that goes right to the base of the horseshoe falls.

8. i bought a book of black-and-white photographs by c.p. evans that was magnificent.

Using Commas and End Punctuation ▪ Add commas and the correct end punctuation as needed in each sentence.

1. What a glorious sight the Falls are

2. Can you imagine going over the Falls

3. People have braved the falls in barrels leaped from platforms and walked across on tightropes

4. Annie Taylor was the first to try a barrel but many others followed

5. One famous tightrope walker stopped sat down and cooked a meal when he was halfway across

6. What a sight that must have been

7. Another famous daredevil was Sam Patch

8. He stood on a platform and leaped thirty metres into the Falls

9. "Theres no mistake in Sam Patch" he said afterward

10. Patch died during another stunt, but the expression became famous

Using Quotation Marks and Apostrophes ■ Add commas, apostrophes, and quotation marks as needed in each sentence.

1. Have you seen Pats new car? asked James.
2. No I havent yet said Diane.
3. What kind did he get? she asked.
4. I dont know for sure said James but I know its red.
5. Diane said How do you know that?
6. He always said thats what hed buy said James.
7. He couldve changed his mind said Diane.
8. James said Not Pat. Hes not the kind of person whod do that.
9. Well said Diane lets go see it now.
10. Lets go! said James.
11. Wow! said Diane. That's a great car!
12. Pat where did you get it? asked James.
13. I got it at the car lot downtown said Pat.

Using Capitalization and Punctuation Correctly ■ Circle each letter that should be capitalized. Add missing commas, periods, quotation marks, and apostrophes. Be sure to write the correct end punctuation in the blank after each sentence.

1309 w. harriman st

antigonish ns b2g 1b4

sept 17 1997

dear shelley

    you wont believe what happened ____ we went to a melodrama, a kind of play, and i became an actor ____ yes its true ____ can fame and fortune be far behind ____ heres what happened ____ we were just sitting there ready to boo the villain when the stage manager came out and asked is there a volunteer in the audience ____ before i knew what was happening, deanna had grabbed my elbow and pushed my hand into the air ____ the stage manager pointed at me and said come on up here and tell us all your story ____

    well i nearly fainted of course but i had no choice ____ so i did it and it was the most fun ive had in a long time ____ i acted out the part of a woman who refuses a heros help ____ he tried to save me from paying rent to a horrible landlord but i took care of him myself ____ then the hero shook my hand and rode off into the sunset ____ it was so funny ____ deanna has pictures and i cant wait to show them to you ____

see you soon

ellen

Writing Sentences ▪ Expand the meaning of each sentence base below. Add adjectives, adverbs, and/or prepositional phrases. Write your expanded sentences.

1. (Geese flew.) _____

2. (Thieves robbed.) _____

3. (Winter approaches.) _____

4. (Doctors treated.) _____

Topic Sentences ▪ Write a topic sentence for the paragraph below.

> My dog and I play ball together. We go on hikes together. My dog is always happy to see me. My dog barks to let me know that a stranger is near. I can teach my dog to obey and to do tricks. I feed and bathe my dog.

TOPIC SENTENCE: _____

Supporting Details ▪ Read the topic sentence below. Then underline the three sentences that contain supporting details.

TOPIC SENTENCE: Finding an apartment takes organization.

1. Look in the newspaper ads for vacant apartments.
2. Driving all over town looking for signs on lawns takes too much time.
3. Check the address to be sure the apartment is in an area you like.
4. Make a list of questions to ask the landlord.
5. Try to remember what each person you talk to says.

Topic and Audience ▪ Circle the audience to whom you would send a letter on each topic below.

1. problems with a new appliance

   a. your family   b. the manufacturer   c. your friends

2. media coverage of local elections

   a. newspaper   b. the mayor   c. the governor

3. concern over rising electric rates

   a. your landlord   b. the electric company   c. your uncle

Clustering ■ Complete the cluster by writing words that the topic in the centre of the cluster relates to. On the line under the cluster, write the audience to whom you would address a paragraph about jobs.

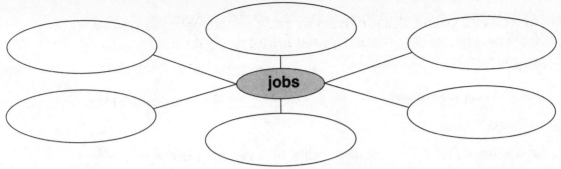

Audience: _____

Writing a Paragraph ■ Now write a paragraph about jobs. Keep the audience you chose in mind. Write a topic sentence and three sentences that contain supporting details. The supporting details may be reasons, facts, or examples.

Jobs

_____

_____

_____

_____

_____

Revising and Proofreading ■ Rewrite the paragraph below. Correct the errors by using the proofreader's marks.

¶ Lakes are bodys of water with land all around⊙ They do not

connect to the the ocean. most lakes contain fresh water, although

a few have salt water. Some very large lakes are called Seas.

_____

_____

_____

_____

_____

Following Directions ▪ Read the directions below. Then number them in the correct order.

_____ 1. Place the pattern on the wood.   _____ 3. Cut along the lines you drew.

_____ 2. Select a piece of wood.   _____ 4. Draw around the pattern.

Alphabetical Order ▪ Read the sample index of a reading book below. Number the boldfaced titles of chapters in alphabetical order. Then number the names of the selections in each chapter in alphabetical order.

INDEX: Types of Reading

_____ **Poems**   _____ **Fiction**

_____ Limericks   _____ The Book of Three

_____ Sonnets   _____ Alice in Wonderland

_____ **Stories of Real People**   _____ **Articles**

_____ Churchill, Man of His Times _____ Violence on Television

_____ The Life of Helen Keller   _____ How to Choose a Good School

Guide Words ▪ Read the guide words for a dictionary page below. Put a check before each entry word that would appear on that page.

1. **eggnog / eject**   2. **harbour / harp**

_____ eggplant   _____ eight   _____ harm   _____ harp

_____ eel   _____ eggbeater _____ hare   _____ happy

Pronunciation ▪ Use the pronunciation key as you look at each respelling. Underline the word that matches the respelling.

1. (sin′ dər)   sender   cinder   single

2. (nā′ shən)   navy   notion   nation

3. (härp)   harm   harp   happy

> hat, āge, fär; let, ēqual, tėrm; it, īce; hot, ōpen, ôrder; oil, out; cup, pùt, rüle; əbove, takən, pencəl, lemən, circəs; ch, child; ng, long; sh, ship; th, thin; ŦH, then; zh, measure

Study Skills

Parts of a Book ■ Write title page, copyright page, table of contents, or index to tell where you would find this information.

_____ **1.** a chapter title

_____ **2.** the page on which certain information
can be found

_____ **3.** the author's name

_____ **4.** the year a book was published

Using an Encyclopedia ■ Read the sample encyclopedia entry below.
Use it to answer the questions that follow.

> **BRAN** is the outer layers of food grains. When flour is made, the outer layers of grain come off. These particles are bran. Bran is a very healthful food. It is full of vitamins and minerals. Bran is used as a breakfast food and as an ingredient in baking. Pure bran is dark brown in colour. Pure bran is often combined with other cereal grains, such as wheat. _See also_ FIBRE and CEREAL.

1. What is the article about? _____

2. What is bran? _____

3. How is bran obtained? _____

4. What colour is pure bran? _____

5. What is a grain that is often combined with pure bran? _____

6. What are the cross-references? _____

Using an Encyclopedia ■ Circle the word you would look under to find an article on each of the following. Then write the number of the volume in which you would find each.

A-C	D-F	G-I	J-L	M-N	O-Q	R-S	T-V	W-Z
1	2	3	4	5	6	7	8	9

_____ **1.** learning how to swim

_____ **2.** St. John's

_____ **3.** dentistry skills

_____ **4.** the life cycle of the ant

_____ **5.** Harriet Tubman

_____ **6.** how syrup is made

_____ **7.** the cause of a yawn

_____ **8.** breeds of cats

Index